UP FROM THE TRAP

Louie T. McClain II

Published by Melanin Origins LLC

PO Box 122123; Arlington, TX 76012

11/11

www.MelaninOrigins.com

First Edition

Library of Congress Control Number: 2019938565

ISBN: 978-1-62676-699-0 hardback

ISBN: 978-1-62676-698-3 paperback

ISBN: 978-1-62676-697-6 ebook

Dedication

This book is for *Emerging Leaders* worldwide.

Also, to *Francis W. Minikon Jr.*

Your legacy proceeds you and your reach extends
to millions. Thank you for your friendship,
mentorship, and unwavering faith in me.

Table of Contents

Foreword

trap
/trap/
noun

1. *a device or enclosure designed to catch and retain animals, typically by allowing entry but not exit or by catching hold of a part of the body.*

2. *a situation in which people lie in wait to make a surprise attack.*

For centuries, African Americans have been placed in cultural, psychological, and economic *traps* and have been unable to identify a successful means of escape.

Because of a culture heavily influenced by hip hop, most people have probably heard of *the trap* or even used the term themselves. However, which definition applies to the state of our people? Artists such as 2 Chainz and T.I. popularized the phrase, but our people's daily entanglement is nothing to sing or dance about. It's dangerous and subtle and can alter lives forever. From the prison system to economic development to daily health options, our growth as a people is slowed by countless well-disguised *traps*. However, we have infinite possibilities and solutions for combatting each one of them. Your perspective, attitude, critical skills, and work ethic will unlock the true potential that resides in us all. This mentality and approach has proven to help individuals not only move *up from the trap*, but also stay out of it and fly above expectations.

Undoubtedly and sometimes unknowingly, we were born in *the trap*. Although some view it as a reference to the hood, the term runs much deeper and affects our psychological development. From movies to music to the systematic development of our living spaces, it is clearer than ever that freedom must be fought for. That simple truth has endured since the beginning of time.

As a people, how do we learn to grow and thrive in an environment that has been designed for hundreds of years with the intent of keeping us from doing so? Once you understand the many traps, obstacles, and barriers that have been systemically engineered to prevent people of color from succeeding in certain ways, you begin to create your own path to freedom. We learn from those who came before us— those who thrived in environments much more treacherous than ours and with fewer resources than we now have at our disposal. When we view the situation in that light, we aren't left with any excuse for falling victim to the same *traps*, no matter how differently they might be set. Through years of community building, mentoring, and progressive professional focus, Louie T. McClain II has concentrated his attention on not only empowering others to move *up from the trap* but also improving perspectives and encouraging people to look inward and around for continuous pushes toward a limitless future filled with opportunities for growth.

With hopes of opening hearts and minds by taking us on a one-of-a-kind journey through the power of his pen, author Louie T. McClain II provides solutions for generations to come.

Each one. Reach one. Teach one. Blessings.

Larry Simmons Jr.

CHANNELING THE GREATNESS
THAT LIES WITHIN

An Aspiration

An Autobiography

An Action Plan

UP FROM THE TRAP

Louie T. McClain II

Rise.

A Rhetorical Question

As the pilot of your own aircraft, you are cruising at the desired altitude as you journey to your next destination.

You have an expectancy to experience many great things at that destination: fun, love, happiness, prosperity, and contentment. Although you have not quite arrived yet – you can still see the joy, smell the aroma, hear the laughter, and feel the warmth.

You know where you are going and you know you will arrive there safely. How do you live your best life today?

Introduction

All my life, I have been searching for the right words, for the right message, and the right platform to reach disadvantaged and disenfranchised people. After doing in depth research on Booker T. Washington, Marcus Garvey, and W.E.B. Du Bois while also undergoing intense life experiences—I have finally arrived at the sum total of my life's work. Booker T. Washington, one of my favorite historical figures, had the brilliance and tenacity to speak to his people and compel them to come *Up From Slavery*. It is my sincere hope that I will be able to add similar value to the lives of all who read this book.

Once and for all, **please allow me to set the record straight:**

The Honorable Booker T. Washington was not a House Negro! Neither was he an Uncle Tom, or a Black Republican (not today's stereotypical version at least), and Mr. Washington was not a man who looked down upon his own people while accommodating or patronizing another. All of his work was for the sake of black people. All of his labor and toil went to benefit his life's work of establishing Tuskegee Normal and Industrial Institute. This is now recognized as Tuskegee University, a thriving Historically

Black College / University (HBCU). What most won't hear is that Booker T. Washington worked for 18 years straight, for the betterment of black people without taking a vacation.

Booker T. was born a slave, but that didn't stop him from ultimately pursuing his goals. He walked over 500 lengthy miles to get an education, and he would sleep on sidewalks due to homelessness for several periods of time. Later on, he worked as a janitor and cleaned toilets to earn his way through college. After earning his way through college, Booker T. eventually went back to his hometown to become a teacher and educate black children.

In the midst of teaching, he was called to teach in Tuskegee, yet he never knew how he would secure funds to provide a quality education for young black boys and girls. This is the life of a man who was completely misunderstood. Many of his own people spoke out against him, and some still do the same today.

This visionary encouraged his people to come Up From Slavery and my only desire is to represent his cause in a thorough manner. Today is a new day! African Americans have experienced numerous disadvantages, such as chattel slavery during the Atlantic Slave Trade, the Jim Crow era, and horribly witnessing the American government dismantle our leaders and organizations. As of now, we still experience mass incarceration and psychological slavery from past trauma. It is time that we come Up From the Trap. What is the trap you say? Simply put, Merriam-Webster defines a trap as

> 1 a: *device for taking game or other animals; especially one that holds by springing shut suddenly*
>
> 2 a: *something by which one is caught or stopped unawares; also a position or situation from which it is difficult or impossible to escape*

Merriam-Webster goes on to provide a few other definitions related to sports and hunting game and it ends its definition listing with this:

6: *any of various devices for preventing passage of something often while allowing other matter to proceed;*

These are the type of definitions one would expect to have seen back in the 90's, but I believe that it's always important to review the etymology and decipher the original intent prior to deep diving into topics. First, it's clear that a trap is not something that someone would want to get caught in. It's something that a person would use to put another at a disadvantage. Another conclusion we can draw is that a trap could be considered as a useful celebratory tool for victors and not the victims. *Sounds about right.* Ok, so let's introduce an alternate concept of a trap. Urban Dictionary's informal definition of Trap is quite simple and plain:

9. *informal*

a place where drugs are sold.

Boom! And there you have it; a place where drugs are sold. Now there is a whole debate (within Black America) on the origin of this word, especially as it pertains to hip hop music. However, I want to look at the actual meaning of the word and how it is currently used in society. The trap has all types of negative connotations... I still have not found a positive one, yet African American culture has embraced it with open arms. I honestly believe that it is time to move on from this phase of our journey. Repurposing the word "trap" is not synonymous to reclaiming the "N" word which was used against blacks and turning it into a term of endearment. It's not the same as celebrating the term "Obamacare" which was coined by those who hated America's first black president.

In this book, *Up From the Trap*, I share with you a few of my life experiences. It paints a picture of what progress should look like for emerging leaders in black America or for any person who desires to have a purpose filled life. Please note that there is no conceit involved in my previous statement and I am choosing my words carefully and humbly. I can tell you that I have a bachelor's degree and that I'm a born again Christian. I have over seven years of full time and volunteer work in Juvenile Justice. I created a non-profit that helped ex-offenders get connected with jobs and I created a college scholarship program for children in Africa. I fought against the system and got full custody of my daughter, I work in corporate America, and most recently – I founded Melanin Origins LLC which provides learning materials (children's books, assessments, and curriculum) to parents and schools about lesser known African American Pioneers.

I can say all these things, but what I really want you to know is that I have walked in so many other shoes. In other words, "my shoe has been on the other foot." For example, I come from a broken family. I was the awkward middle child and saw my dad about once a year. I was bullied in elementary school. I was in a gang in high school and started smoking at age 14 and drinking at age 15. Smoking five blunts of marijuana a day was normal for me when I was a kid. I sold drugs for a couple years. I had my share of girls, fights, drugs, and a few shootouts. I was actively involved in few drive-bys too. I've been kicked out of school and my own home. All of my friends went to jail or prison. I paid half of my way through college only to be fired from my first real career gig. I've experienced unemployment, and I have two kids from two women.

I can go on and on about my list of flaws along with my list of successes. I am sharing this message with you because I am a human being with imperfections, and at the same time I have found the key to making a way out of no way. What I am about to share with you is the blueprint to how our communities can thrive once again; not only like how we did centuries ago in Egypt (which many of our leaders seem to *only* discuss), but just as how we were extremely prosperous and successful 100 years ago with Black Wall Streets in Tulsa, Oklahoma and Wilmington, North Carolina. This is how we put an end to the issues that we are currently fighting. This is how we succeed in living in racial harmony. Most importantly, this is how we attain happiness and put an end to the endless pursuit of it.

CHAPTER ONE

The Root

A s plainly stated in the Urban Dictionary, the *trap* is a place where drug dealers and other hustlers meet and hang out to engage in criminal activity. The most notable criminal activity that takes place in the trap is the sale of illegal drugs. Other activities that occur in the trap or a "trap house" include:

- Cooking / manufacturing drugs
- Doing drugs
- Prostitution
- Harboring illegal weapons
- And a slew of other organized criminal activity.

According to a 2017 article from ThoughtCo., "Trap music is a style of hip-hop that sprung out of the southern rap scene in the 1990s. Trap took its root in Atlanta, where the likes of Ghetto Mafia and Dungeon Family first used the term to describe their sound."

Underground Kingz (UGK) had also been major proponents of mentioning the trap in their lyrics as well. For the

2 | UP FROM THE TRAP

record, rapper T.I. states that he created the term "trap music" even though the word "trap" already existed, and was used by artists to describe the drug dealing lifestyle.

Today, the *trap* still signifies the actual physical location of a drug house, but it is incredulously held at high regard in the African-American community as it has become more than just a place for illegal activity. Take note that the type of illegal activity referred to here is the type of activity that has been destroying families for years. These concepts flood the radio waves, permeates our social media and television feeds, and are seen everywhere we turn. It holds the spotlight in music, fashion, and business advertisements. Yet, history has shown us that young men and women head into a cycle of drug addiction which ultimately leads to their incarceration for drug offenses.

Why is trap a big deal anyway?

Today's "hip-hop" and R&B music openly promotes date rape, assault and battery, murder, aggravated assault, kidnapping and overall irresponsible living. This discourages hard work, the family unit and ultimately, what it takes for true progress in our communities. Artists, regardless of race, are highly encouraged to make this type music (breed or perpetuate this type of culture) and have very limited restrictions in promoting the criminal lifestyle over radio waves. What was once seen as a way out of poverty (displaying artistic talent and receiving compensation for it) is now polluted by the same group of people it was created by and for. Legendary pioneers who have found great success in the hip-hop industry also enjoy the evolution of today's rap music. (Trap music)

Producer and rapper Sean "Diddy" Combs, formerly known as Puff Daddy, Puffy, P. Diddy, and now just "Diddy", made this statement via twitter in regards to the 2018 Grammy nominations,

> *"Hip Hop was seen as a non-priority in the 90s, it was seen as a genre of music that wouldn't last. It was so raw and infectious that it broke out of just being a trend and became the culture."*

Furthermore, Diddy went on to say this in another tweet months later,

> *"If we don't own our culture then we have nothing!!! You think we have nothing now. We must own our culture! It's not negotiable!!! The culture that we created will be our first real opportunity to gain economic wealth as a people. We must work together because we all we got!!"*

Now don't get me wrong, I believe Mr. Combs is harping the right tune when he makes a reference to ownership, economic wealth, and the influence that music has on culture. However, what artists such as Diddy miss is while it is a good thing to use your God given talents to produce revenue for yourself . . . the ends do not justify the means . . . and even more so when you're considering the greater good of the community. The real issue is that trap culture has infected the black community to the point where trap is taken so seriously that it is extremely difficult for it to be uprooted from our daily lives. It's in our attitudes, behaviors, and worst of all . . . it's in our mind as something that just is which, by default, makes it something that is acceptable. It is accepted as a social norm in our community, not necessarily selling illegal drugs, but embracing the thoughts, behaviors, and ideologies of the most troubled kind. Trap says it's ok to cut corners, drop out of school to participate in illegal activity, and that it's ok to not seek to be your best self. This is, personally, my fundamental problem with the whole matter.

A very wise sister I know uses the phrase, "Word. Sound. Power." to describe the ways today's modern media is used to inform, misinform, and dis-inform the people. Of course print media holds great power, but she affirms that your words pretty much mean nothing until they are spoken. The spoken words produce sounds that others will be able to hear and if those sounds (spoken words) are rehearsed again and again, especially by authoritative figures, then eventually people will begin to believe it. That is where Power lies: *word, sound, power.* You know, it's the thought that the person with the loudest voice in the room prevails.

In the Spring of 2016, Fort Worth, Texas native Go-Yayo (yayo is a term used to describe cocaine [The movie Scarface: "Che Che get the yayo"]) participated in a middle school pep rally in the Fort Worth Independent School District. Yes, a young man who has drugs as part of his alias was invited to a grade school. Go-Yayo's raps are about violence, drugs, and blatant disrespect toward women. While some kids can relate to his background, his words put him in a position of "power" and now he's a sought out individual.

How about this: whether you believe in global warming or not, the only way that you know that it exists is because someone seemingly important coined the phrase and now scholars and scientists have been debating it for decades now. Here is another example: President Barack Obama was not born in the United States of America; the infamous lie that was conjured up by prejudice individuals in an attempt to thwart President Obama's candidacy for office. Once that lie was created, it was repeated over and over again until many individuals began believing it. This lie was widely perpetuated as truth until President Obama finally came forth with his birth certificate affirming his American citizenship.

If I may divert into a theological explanation, words mean *everything* to those who acknowledge the spiritual world. Whether we're speaking about the law of attraction— the ability to attract the things that you constantly think about, speak about, and pursue—or the fact that the Creator established the Universe simply by speaking words, it is certainly prudent to consider the power of words when monitoring the messages you allow into your body. I believe that these are universal principles, but I will use the Bible as a reference. Here are a few examples:

1. God created the heavens and Earth by saying "let there be light" etc.

2. The Holy Trinity is composed of three elements: Father, Word, & the Holy Spirit. Most individuals shortcut the truth by affirming Father, Son, and Holy Spirit, but John 1:1 says – "in the beginning was the Word, and the Word was with God, and the word *was* God. The same was in the beginning with God. All things were made by Him." It is clear that the words that were spoken ever since the beginning of time are powerful! So much so that God equates His word with His own self.

3. When Jesus was tempted by Satan while in the wilderness—he quoted God's word and that is how he overcame the enemy. He was filled with good direction and positive messages so much so that he could endure dangerous situations.

4. The book of Romans admonishes new believers who desire to live a better lifestyle to be transformed by the renewing of their minds which is done by continuously hearing and reading the word.

5. There are dozens of more examples of this but I'll use this one. The book of Hebrews says that believers overcame the evil one by

    a. the blood of the lamb (Jesus Christ) and

    b. the WORD of their testimony.

My basic understanding of the bible is to view the stories and letters within the appropriate historical context. I take the writer and who the writer was actually writing to into consideration. Then I determine the spiritual meaning (what God is trying to convey to the reader), and lastly… I make it practical for everyday living. I think it is fair for us to conclude that words do have power. It is the duty of words to feed into our psyche and seek to become our reality.

Side note: here is where a dissenter will chime in about systematic oppression and how one can be a product of one's environment. They will say that we, Africans in the diaspora, were placed in a disadvantaged state and that the forces are too great for us to overcome. Well… I mostly agree with that sentiment, because the argument is partly right. The problem lies in the fact that we all *can* overcome. We all just need to move in the right direction and *trap* is the wrong direction.

I began with politics and I have spoken about religion, but coming up from the trap doesn't mean that we only revert to those two options. Coming up from the trap is about experiencing a true quality of life. This is about economics, generational wealth, and unity among races. It's about achievement and outdoing the naysayers *and* those who oppose our ultimate freedom. Lastly, this is about honoring the family unit and rearing generations of successful children who will do the same in return. If we indeed want to witness these great things – we must first acknowledge the detrimental effect that trap culture has on our community.

I have found that the greatest leaders of the African American community believed in:

1. Education
2. Working for the betterment of the black community
3. Raising the standard within the black community

We can clearly see this thread in the exhortations and admonishments of Booker T. Washington, W.E.B. Du Bois, and Marcus Garvey. Even though they did not always agree with each other, they all still found a way to address the quality of life conditions, morals, attitudes, and social ethics of the people. *I hope we get the proper context...* Frederick Douglass, who fought in the Union Army against the Confederacy, stood face to face with fellow blacks and admonished them about the proper ways of living. Booker T. Washington, who was born a slave, made it his life's work to labor on behalf of the black community and he also admonished them about the best ways to experience success (hard work and a true sense of community).

Du Bois and Garvey, two opposing gentlemen from two different worlds of the black experience labored intensely on the behalf of black people, yet they also called out what they perceived as lack, slack, and foolishness among black people. So let's not forget or get it twisted – we must hold ourselves accountable. If we desire change and progress, we must understand that, for today's time, we must come up from the trap! Certain things that are done against black people are done directly with evil intent and maliciousness such as lynching (yes, it still occurs in the 21st Century), police violence, hurling racial slurs, and targeted acts of terror. For example, the Austin Bombings of 2018 was specifically directed toward affluent African-Americans in Austin, Texas. Additionally, African Americans regularly experience injustice through discriminatory housing policies, mass incarceration, high police presence in inner cities due to flawed policy and legislation, and the vicious school to prison pipeline to name a few. It is our job to fight, vehemently, to close all loopholes in these systems. Again – it is OUR job. Not the job of another race, creed, or nationality. We must be able to do these things for ourselves. What does that process look like though?

Here's the television version of that process: A person meets their partner. They work in today's capitalistic society to make ends meet. They are enjoying each other's company and the fruits of their labor. They decide marriage is the next step in their relationship, so they get married and have children. The children grow up seeing their parent's love for each other, respect for the family unit, and the children are encouraged to aspire to be the best academically. Thus the cycle perpetuates into the "American Dream." Allow me to add a few more intricacies to paint a better picture.

Let's say the couple both work for a major corporation or a local business. Either way – they recognize that two incomes are better than one. Finding love and compatibility is a struggle in and of itself, but in the picture I'm painting... the couple understands the value in it. Marriage is a very big and important step, not only in relationships, but in one's own quality of life and in fostering a better community. In the picture I'm painting, the married couple has a trade, they have an education, and they are also working toward plans that will uplift their community. There are many ways it could be accomplished too. They can:

1. Volunteer minimal hours at a local community organization
2. Host neighborhood cleanup projects
3. Create a non-profit to aid the needy in the community
4. Create a business to employ the community
5. Lead charitable and selfless lives that encourage love, respect, community involvement, and much more.

The things that I am mentioning here is nothing new and it is not uncommon to find shining stars in each major city in the U.S that are holding fast to these practices. The problem is that now our community is saturated with so many conflicting messages that we seemingly have forgotten that collective progression is the best way forward. We think that individualism, in the respect of only focusing on one's self or one's family, is how we'll overcome the plunder of racism and discrimination. Somehow we have been fooled to believe that so long as *I* do whatever it takes just for *me* to shine, whether legally or illegally, *I* have made myself a success and that's all that matters, but I beg to differ. The true measure of an individual is by the ways in which his character and his actions impact the lives of others. After Slavery we experienced the Jim Crow era. After Jim Crow then mass incarceration, and everything that makes one complicit to become incarcerated is what is preached to our children every day of their lives through music, television, and through watching the "sheeple" do what they do best. We must come up from this trap.

This goes far beyond the pull up your pants movement. It also goes way further than boycotting rap music. This *(coming up from the trap)* reach stretches way past the need for a spiritual awakening among the people. Coming up from the trap incorporates the idea that we are equally capable of doing anything that any man can do. Whether we were here before European settlers or brought here by them against our will, the fact remains that we are resilient and unstoppable people. We can build our own, we can educate our own, and we can thrive in current businesses and institutions. We can do all of that with excellence. Should we make the conscious decision to reject what is plotted out for us through the trap then we can certainly experience true equity and equality (en masse) while living in the United States.

Imagine what things would have been like if we all continued, in our own way, to move toward mutual progress. Just imagine that! Booker T. revolutionized and brought hope, change, literacy, and commerce to the little town of Tuskegee. And those who followed Du Bois could have been the lawyers and civil rights activists taking up the fight for change through legislation and direct action. Washington and Du Bois did not have to have public disagreements. The hand may operate differently from the foot, but the body works together toward one common goal – self-preservation. But we have lost that as a community focus and have knelt down and accepted it solely on an individualistic level. Slaves were killed for wanting to experience a better life! Many pro-voters, sharecroppers, local businessmen, civil rights activists, and countless others who wished to witness a better life for themselves and for people who look like them experienced the same plight as well.

******

The Trap adversely affects the community as a whole in many ways. It promotes drug usage, robbery, rape, murder, other forms of assault and violence, and it breeds poverty and illiteracy. It encourages short-cuts while actively discouraging hard work. It promotes individualism and getting rich by any means but it does not promote positive community involvement, etc. Rather than providing a three-point message on the topic… I can sum it up with this one statement: trap culture is leading the community into economic powerlessness. No economic power means no voice whatsoever. History teaches us that tyranny is inevitable; government conquering government is inevitable; tables do turn. Just how exactly does our community, being fully ingrained in trap culture, expect to have a true voice at the polls, in the office, at the board meetings, and in the political experience? We must do our best to establish our economic power, because simply having funds is not enough. Using our funds to better our condition collectively is where power lies. Other ethnic groups practice this type of thinking in their cultures and lifestyles and find great success.

Look at quality of life of Asian Americans. Pew Research Center concludes,

> *Asians are projected to become the largest immigrant group in the country, surpassing Hispanics in 2055. The median annual household income of households headed by Asian Americans is $73,060, compared with $53,600 among all U.S. households. About half of Asians ages 25 and older (51%) have a bachelor's degree or more, compared with 30% of all Americans this age.*

Let's measure these statistics against African Americans shall we. While Pew Research Center reports that,

> *"A growing share of blacks are completing high school and college. For the first time in U.S. history, 90% of Americans ages 25 and older have completed high school. It still remains that black households have only 10 cents in wealth for every dollar held by white households."*

The point of these statistics is not to talk down on my own people or to disregard or negate the impacts of systemic racism. The point here is that, if you live in America, you know without a shadow of a doubt that no other culture openly celebrates and practices self-destruction and call it culture as seen with trap culture. Is this the sole determinant for any ethnic groups success? Not at all! There still remains a systemic beast that must be defeated, but ridding ourselves of trap culture is a good, monumental step in the right direction. Mexican Americans do their best to hold fast to their traditions and their ethic of hard work and community and within a decade or two they (Hispanic-Americans) will be the majority in the U.S. How much collective power do you think they will have then? Once again, the purpose in evaluating other people groups is for us to see what is working and to also identify what is not working.

The root of trap culture has been identified and exposed for what it is at a fundamental level. The root of the trap, as our culture knows it, is drug dealing and the lifestyle it breeds: pure, malicious criminal activity. Here's the trap in a hand basket: poverty stricken young men and women with incredible talent receive money to perpetuate lifestyles that are completely detrimental to the community. We have allowed them (celebrities) to set this standard, but the celebrity is in a position where their boss (who doesn't care about the community) sets this standard as well. What is clear is that the people in the background, media executives, do not care about the community. While they are passing along these destructive messages and lifestyles... they are also giving their corporate cronies in the prison industry a reason to point and laugh. Yes, "look at how they destroy themselves... all for the love of money" is the talk after the boardroom meetings. "They think this will save them, but they don't know that they can save themselves. We will keep them dependent on us, and we will not come to their aid when they actually carry out these lifestyles and are killed in the street justly or unjustly. They have acknowledged and accepted the standard that we have set for them."

CHAPTER TWO

The Internal Issue

Not only should our community rise up from the trap due to its root and innate negative connotation, but we also need to come up from owning it as our culture at large. The average person knows that the United States government is responsible for bringing cocaine directly into inner cities. After that, the government purposely turned a blind eye on the usage and sale of those drugs for just enough time to witness thriving communities become destroyed. When violent crimes, overdoses, and births of drug addicted-babies began shooting up at alarming rates, the government then decided to declare a war on drugs. This so-called "war on drugs" wrongly portrayed African-American males as criminal perpetrators. This subsequently caused tens of thousands of black men to be targeted, arrested, and incarcerated.

So why are we celebrating this nonsense? Why are we making an attempt to paint that scenario as if it is, or was, a good thing to happen to us? The sale and usage of illegal drugs, and all the negativity that spawns from it, is not something for any respectable people to own and claim as their culture. This trap lifestyle should not be internalized, but that's what we're allowing to be a reality for our children. Here are a few problems with internalizing and celebrating trap culture:

1. The pressure of social and economic success is already too immense for our black and brown children
2. It discourages the family unit
3. It breeds consumer culture and not ownership culture

When we celebrate trap lifestyle, what messages are we sending to our children? We are telling them that their sole focus should be on gaining material things. We are telling them to put their security in the things that they possess, and that is an inadequate way to prepare a child for the real world. Through default, we are teaching our children that they, alone, are not good enough; that it's what they have to show, externally, that determines their value. Sadly, we are displaying to our youth that luxurious quantities are more important than intrinsic human qualities.

Clearly this is not good because there are hosts of children in our community who don't have parents that are able to provide a luxurious lifestyle for their kids. This easily leads to a superiority complex in the children whose parents do have the funds to support that lifestyle and an inferiority complex in the children whose parents don't. I absolutely understand that some parents do have the means to provide their children with the finer things in life, and I have no problem with that. But trap lifestyle is a problem because it takes attaining the finer things in life to another level. For kids, it could lead to bullying and low self- esteem if they don't have what the trap lifestyle prescribes.

Example: According to trap, if you don't have material things to show then you're broke. If you're broke then you're a loser. If you're a loser then you have no future and you need to do whatever illegal activities there are to ensure that you are not considered broke. Also, according to trap culture, if you're broke then you're undesirable by the opposite sex and you are deemed as weak.

This type of reasoning is drenched throughout trap music and those who have parents who cannot afford such things feel pressure to get those excessive material items by any means necessary. Rob someone? Sure, go ahead. Sell drugs to your own community and even family members? Yes! Burglarize another's property and be ready to kill them if they catch you too? Damn skippy!

We are erring! We are erring majorly! We constantly listen to music that promotes this lifestyle and then we wonder why our children begin to emulate this lifestyle. We wonder why other communities look down on us. Yes, there is a great amount of successful African-Americans who don't ascribe to these messages; but there is an even larger amount of us who have not escaped the harsh reality of life and these messages (coupled with a vicious system of racism) keep them bound.

The media has a firm grip on these individuals, and it oversaturates them with destructive content. Then we, as consumers, turn right around and promote that lifestyle as if we're proving a point that we're rich or able to "Keep up with the Jones'." We do these things, all while getting the same negative results on the job, in the court house, by the housing authority, and by the education system. We have ascribed to the trap and have fallen for their trap. And we seem to do it willingly as well. Just so we're clear, gaining financial wealth is good, materialistic riches are fine, and building generational wealth is optimally best. The problem that is being discussed here is the die hard, burn every bridge, capitalistic greed mentality. When it comes to trap culture, those who are not strongly encouraged to resort to criminal or deviant behavior are simply encouraged to funnel their aspirations through a few select channels: sports, acting, or music.

Growing up in the African-American community, I noticed that many children who desired to play sports mainly focused on playing basketball or football. And many children, who loved music, primarily focused on hip-hop, R&B, and the production thereof. Now, all of these professions are noble ones and take a great amount of skill, dedication, creativity, and grit to be successful in each endeavor. However, this is dangerous for a couple reasons. The first reason is because each and every human being was born with a unique purpose. We all have unique skills, burdens, and talents that we've inherited or acquired over some time. And many of us, especially our children, have not gotten to the point in our life's journey where we've gotten to know or understand who we are or our purpose for being. Trap lifestyle takes the place of reason, and provides a bunch of negative and discouraging guidance. In essence, trap stunts our ability to grow and create.

The second reason is that it is simply irrational for a large sum of people to all funnel into a few small select fields of opportunity.

A recent NCAA study concluded:

Men's Basketball

- High school senior players who go on to play NCAA men's basketball: Less than one in 35, or 2.9 percent.

- NCAA senior players drafted by an NBA team: Less than one in 75, or 1.3 percent.
- High school senior players eventually drafted by an NBA team: About three in 10,000, or 0.03 percent.

Football

- High school senior players who go on to play NCAA men's football: About one in 17, or 5.8 percent.
- NCAA senior players drafted by an NFL team: About one in 50, or 2.0 percent.
- High school senior players eventually drafted by an NFL team: About nine in 10,000, or 0.09 percent.

The NCAA study concluded:

Sadly though, it comes as a rude surprise to many athletes yearning for a professional sports career to learn that the odds against success are astronomically high. Approximately 1 percent of NCAA men's basketball players and 2 percent of NCAA football players are drafted by NBA or NFL teams—and just being drafted is no assurance of a successful professional career. "Student-athletes" whose sole and now failed objective was to make the pros suddenly find themselves in a world that demands skills their universities did not require them to learn.

It appears that the NCAA is being clear when it comes to the odds of ultimate success in sports. As parents and community leaders, can we not be clear with ourselves for the sake of our children as well? The system that we have been operating under has failed for quite some time now... and a little bit too long if you ask me. It is time that we uproot and come up from the trap, but it begins with our decision to resolve to do so. Too much pressure is placed on our children to be of poor character. When they continue to get the negative results that the laws of nature have ordained for negative behavior, it will be us to blame for allowing them to continue down that destructive path. We discussed earlier that parents may not be able to provide a materialistic lifestyle for their children while some can; but there's still the bully element that is embedded in trap lifestyle. Another point to consider is that a vast amount of Americans live in poverty.

Although the U.S Census Bureau reports show that the average median income was $59,039 in 2016, Social Security's National Average Wage Index reports, "By definition, 50 percent of wage earners had net compensation less than or equal to the median wage, which is estimated to be $30,533.31 for 2016." About half of the families in the U.S. bring in an income that is half of what the average American family earns. Furthermore, some 2016 poverty thresholds were:

- $12,486 for a single individual under age 65
- $14,507 a household of two people with a householder 65 years or older with no children
- $24,339 for a family of four with two children under age 18

To add a little more clarity here, Pew Research Center compiled research about America's middle class and found, "By its definition, a household of three would have to earn between $42,000 and $125,000 to qualify as middle-class." Question: do you know a single mother with two or three children? How well do you think she fares when gauging these numbers?"

As for me, my heart almost melted when I learned such a vast amount of Americans gross under $30k yearly. Our children are no richer than us, yet, we are still itching after trap culture. We have greatly missed the mark by choosing to internalize it. Our children fight the same battles we fought and still lose to the same enemy. Now there is an enemy who is without (external) and there is an enemy that is within (internal), and in order to defeat the opposer of all the good things, African-Americans must rise up from the trap.

******

Not only is there immense pressure on our kids, but owning trap lifestyle has contributed to the continued degradation of the family unit. Now, let's take the pressure off of ourselves for a second to deeply analyze something that I once swore (through ignorance) to keep out of my conversation: *slavery*. As the Honorable Mr. Booker T. Washington proposed in his autobiography—we must come up from slavery, however, in doing so we must acknowledge the pain, the impacts, and the continued effect that slavery *still* has on black people in America. Again, there was a point in my life when I only wanted to focus on results and making the best of what I have *now* so that I can have a successful tomorrow. I believed I could leave slavery out of the conversation. . . . Boy I was wrong.

Hill Harper wrote a book in 2009 called "The Conversation." This book was mainly about romantic relationships, but it provided an analytical deep-dive on African-American relationships. It showed how black people in America had the worst rates and percentages when it came to relationships through statistics. For instance, blacks have the highest divorce rates, lowest marriage rates, highest single parent home percentages (predominantly female), and highest child out of wedlock rates. I was astonished when I read the numbers, but even more perplexed when Mr. Harper introduced the concept of slavery to provide the reasoning behind all the madness. I was greatly enlightened after reading Mr. Harper's literature.

Black people are the only people in America to be uprooted from their home country, language, culture, and taken into another land in chains and shambles all to be forced to work for no compensation. They were also not allowed to practice their religion or speak their native languages. Ok, yes we know this about slavery right? But let's have some sanctity and reverence the pain, suffering, and untold despair experienced by those individuals. Again, Africans were brought to foreign lands and sold as property. If a husband, mother, and child had the opportunity to remain with their family up until that time that would've been a rare blessing, but based off documented evidence we know that was not the case in most circumstances. As property, some slaves were allowed to marry and some were not. Many, who were allowed to marry, found their partner on the plantation they lived on and others found their partner on a nearby plantation.

On each plantation, however, the master had his way, so if a slave was unpleasant to the master—he could have him beat, killed, or sold. He could also have his choice of any slave woman whom he desired. Imagine being in the position of a male slave witnessing the continuous flirtatious spirit of the slave owner against a female slave counterpart. Imagine having to hold your tongue while your sister or wife is being raped and treated as mere meat. In most cases, that's all a male slave could do— watch, as any self-determinative action would result in death.

You see, because of this unfortunate situation of repetitive experiences, Harper contends that black women *subconsciously* learned long ago that they could not trust or rely on black men simply due to our position in society. But Louie, slaves were emancipated over 200 years ago. True, but white supremacy still holds a lot of power in the American governmental system. This system has held this power since slavery and has brought further subjugation and discrimination to people of color. I'm not going to deep dive into the gruesome details of lynchings, tar feathering, tying slaves to horses facing opposite directions and whooping them so that they dash off ripping the slave to shreds, and all the other acts of murder that slave masters were able to carry out with impunity. No, this conversation is not about that deep dive, but I will say that immediately after the slaves were freed is when the slave patrols took prominence. From slavery, to slave patrols, to Jim Crow laws and segregation, to the fight for civil rights, to the war on drugs, and even up until today's time of mass incarceration; the stigma of slavery and simply being black in America puts black people at the helm of heinous, unfair treatment causing psychological trauma and broken communities.

Did you notice what I did there? I spoke a little about slavery and then zoomed through 200 years and brought us back to today. Within those 200 years black people have fought to be considered equal and receive just treatment under the constitution of this country. Even leading up to mass incarceration of today (which is a stronghold on the African-American community mainly due to drug offenses), what we must realize is that the thread had always been the same. Disrupt the family unit and the community will not thrive. Make the women not trust or be able to rely on the man. Kill him, lock him up, assassinate his character, black ball him, make it to where it is extremely difficult for him to be gainfully employed, etc. The mold has been the same. Consider social welfare if you will. It is a great tool that's designed to be temporary and for families in need of assistance to get on their feet, but the way the system is set up now... a woman can receive free housing or pay a small fraction of the true price if she has kids and is unmarried. She can get hundreds of dollars a month in food stamps, receive daycare vouchers, get government assistance for higher education and a slew of benefits *if* she does not have a husband or claim a male provider in her household.

Women are far more intelligent than men. They have learned that there are many power move options available to them in this part of the world regardless of skin color. These power moves are available to them as long as they do not allow a man to get in the way of their benefits, so, essentially, Uncle Sam steps in just as the slave master did back the day. There is still a system in place that desires to cripple the family unit and the African-American man, but since we have full knowledge of our past and how it has impacted us for generations, we can now make a change for a better tomorrow.

Many of us get into debates with each other about these conversations and it's so black and white that it's ridiculous. It's either, slavery and systematic oppression are the cause of all things that are wrong with black culture and ultimately... there is nothing we can do to come out of it but take small strides, protest, and continue to fight in the same way we've been fighting. Or it's personal responsibility and free will are king. The latter argument holds that each person has the ability, as an individual, to choose to win or lose in this game of life. Clearly, both opinions are polar opposites and not 100% true, but if we can simply admit that then we can commit to successfully waging war on both fronts.

In waging war, we must realize that we are currently in the best position ever to fight and win this war against the system, but at the same time we must choose to wage war within ourselves first. We must collectively choose to come up from the trap!

Although it is not reflected in our inner cities and in various statistics, in reality, African-Americans are in the best position that we've ever been in because the U.S. Constitution has been modernized. What was written hundreds of years ago about all men being created equal, is practiced in better fashion today (no chattel slavery, major strides have been made for civil rights, gay marriage is legal, etc.). Also, there are no segregation laws and affirmative action still abounds. Yes, it is true that, due to continued discrimination and unequal access to capital and learning materials, African-Americans still need affirmative action to have opportunities that they wouldn't have been privy to otherwise. With that being said, we have the ability to hone in on the benefits of affirmative action and rise to the ranks in our career fields. We can do that and create change within those companies and institutions.

As African-Americans, we can also build our own businesses and institutions. We can do that and compete with current business structures.

Today African-Americans have over one trillion dollars of buying power. You mean to tell me that we collectively share over one trillion dollars, yet we are some of the greatest *consumers* on the planet? Obviously, bills must get paid and there is nothing wrong with having nice things, but what are we doing with those funds in regards to bettering our collective quality of life and advancing our causes? We can easily have a stake in all elements of America in the pursuit of happiness if we can convince ourselves to come up from the trap. Internalizing trap lifestyle is greatly detrimental to our children because of the unneeded strain and unrealistic pressure that it places on them and it also discourages the family unit. Without family, there is no core, no true masculine/feminine balance. This produces lack in generational wealth, collective community advancement, and our ability to create our own institutions. The opportunity to fight the good fight and win exists and it is solely up to us to move on it.

CHAPTER THREE

The External Force

I n the last two chapters, we've discussed the root of Trap
and the problem with internalizing it or owning it as a
way of life. Now we're diving into the main reason why
black people should flee trap lifestyle immediately. On the
macro level . . . trap lifestyle is simply a tool used by those
who hate liberty, equality, and equity to control the masses.

1. It's already fulfilling its purpose in keeping Americans
   ignorant of what it takes to attain true economic
   power and financial freedom.
2. It's crippling us financially.
3. It's a mere tool of distraction

The sum total of my journey through life has taught
me that knowledge is the key to life. It is the key to abundance,
getting ahead, and the first step in accomplishing your every
desire. People simply have to *know* what their passion in life is.
After that, they need to learn and understand the process of
working on their passion. Lastly and most importantly, they
need to know how to master that process. People should also
take time to get to know who they are. Once they find this

key piece of knowledge then they will know that they can achieve all of their dreams.

In terms of the trap, that integral piece of knowing who you are, is completely lost, discarded, and/or distorted to the point where the proponents of trap culture are heavily callous to their true nature and abilities. Before I dive deeper into the Macro Plan for trap culture which is imposed by external forces, I want to circle back to knowledge. We have to understand that knowledge is gained through the process of education. Preaching to the choir—I know, but trust me, there is a reason why I must say what we already know. The sad part is that we have taken a gloriously useful word such as education and made it blunt, boring, and mundane in the ears of our children. Some of our children view education as a task, a punishment, and as something they are doing just to be doing. They're not grasping the true value of it, yet education is all about understanding your potential and knowing how to lead and get ahead in life. Education helps us find these qualities within ourselves.

******

What I want you to understand is that trap is drug dealing. That lifestyle is the exact opposite of the happy, fruitful, and prosperous life that we desire for our community if internalized. At the same time, no matter how much we internalize it, we must understand that trap culture is actually being imposed on our community by outside forces. For the most part, these outside forces either hate our very existence or are too money hungry to deal with the cognitive dissonance that cries out to their psyche as they feed people poison for profit.

Now let's be clear, because a few things are often taken out of context . . . money is *not* the root of all evil. Money has many forms and is simply a tool used for bartering. Don't get me wrong now, having a lot of money does mean that you have the ability to have more materialistic things than a person who may lack funds. I've heard that the golden rule is: he who has the gold makes the rules. So I'm not going to pretend as if money is not important or that having plenty of money (riches / wealth) is not something to be desired. What is true, however, is that the love of money is the root of all evil. Loving money so much in pursuit of whatever (power, sexual love, land, respect, etc.) is the root of all evil. If you love this inanimate object so much – it could lead you to steal from or defraud others just to obtain it. It could lead you to kill another human being for it. It could cause you to enslave an entire nation for your prosperous endeavors. It could cause you to set up systems whereby only your friends or people who look like you can win and it could cause others to be disenfranchised all because you, with the gold, have made the rules.

I definitely don't want to preach to anyone about good and evil. I only want us, as a community, to put this whole trap / money thing into perspective. Can't you see it? Trap: let's do something illegal (perceivably evil) such as selling drugs to humans (my race, your race . . . doesn't matter). Let's do this and not allow anyone else to interfere with the money we're getting from such illegal enterprises. If the police try to stop us then we will lie to them or even kill them if we have to. If others from the competition want to interfere with our cash flow then we'll forcefully show them who runs the show. We'll kill them, kill their babies and grandmothers, we'll kidnap their daughters and cut off body parts. We'll rape their mothers. We'll promote the usage of these drugs to our own people and even encourage them to live exactly how we live. We'll teach them how to cook drugs through song. We'll teach them how to date rape women and build a criminal empire too. Now I must digress. . . I've already touched on internalizing trap culture and I've already acknowledged the systematic efforts that are in place to hold African-Americans and other minority groups in a perpetual state/cycle of dependency and self-insufficiency.

My contention is this: our culture has internalized something that we know stems from the evil of all evils, trap; a plan that was set up against us. My question is this: if we know that this whole thing was *and* is being setup against us . . . why are we continuing to embrace it? Ok, perhaps it's still unclear that trap lifestyle is a part of systematic oppression. Allow me to provide some light on the matter then. I'll begin by posing a few questions: What do most African-American children want to become when they grow up? Answer: an athlete, thespian, or musical artist. What images do they see about African-Americans in visual media? Let's see . . . rappers, NFL players, NBA players, Beyoncé, they see stories of Trayvon Martin, Ferguson, Missouri, Sandra Bland, Tamir Rice, etc. What do inner city youth see when they step outside their houses? Government housing, heavy police presence, drug dealers, torn down neighborhoods, gangs and other criminal activity, etc. Granted, these children might be in pursuit of something fun or innocent when they step outside of their homes such as walking to school, wanting to play outside, or heading to get some groceries or candy, but these are some daily realities for children who live in such conditions. This is the experience for a majority of black children in America. Think about it . . . when children turn on the radio what are they hearing? Here's one: "Scotty too hottie, put the lil' b*tch on the molly, she f*cks everybody." And the asterisk is exactly what it is... a small bleep with just enough consonance emphasis so that the listener can hear the intended message clearly. How about this, "Percocet, Molly, Percocet" in Future's Mask Off. Here's another one from Lil Wayne's Throwed Off freestyle, "Blood Gang Bitch... Bullets fuck your body up... Murk your pussy ass... kidnap the baby and the fuckin babysitter."

Even movies that portray criminal lifestyles as a positive thing will most likely have the bad guy in a dire negative position at the end of the movie if he's not dead already. But the current state of our music is overly saturated with negative and destructive imagery and messages for our people, let alone our children. The question to ask now is—why? Why is this the dominant theme when it comes to the black community? Country music has different themes and so does rock and roll, folk, and bluegrass, but artists in these genres wouldn't dare to plainly tell their consumers to openly conduct a murderous/date rape lifestyle in such a repetitive manner. It appears that the dominant music of black culture is the only one with such destructive themes . . . why is that? If your answer is racism or the system of racism, then I'd like for you to elevate that thought. Do your research to see how and why the system of racism is a tool that is used by those who hold the gold. He who has the gold makes the rules right? It's a tool. We will remain as the working, lower level class until we understand the forces that are working against us, until we know ourselves and the power that we possess, and until we decide to do something about it. Now I could have said until we collectively do something about it, but that would cause inaction by individuals until the greater sum of us decided, as a collective, to begin to act. But it remains . . . we have to recognize these things and decide to do something about it.

In today's world, the solutions are no longer found solely in marching and protesting, it is not found in burning and looting, and it is not 100% found in boycotting, sabotage, or any other means. I believe we can find multiple solutions in different ways, but first, we must fully understand this conversation that we're having right now. As I mentioned before, the systems that are in place are not all for the good of the black community. The system desires to keep us stagnant and destructive toward one another and it desires to prove to others that black people are inferior savages. This is done for one reason only—*the system of white supremacy wants and continues to capitalize off it.* That is it! This is the main reason why individual success from the black race is not sufficient. We must go back and educate the masses of our people to pull them up from the trap, because . . . this is a *trap* and for some reason . . . the main ones who are receiving the short end of the stick are the main ones celebrating "trap lifestyle." This must change!

Some of you might say, "Not everyone who is involved in the entertainment business is out to perpetuate this cycle of destruction." To that I say this: I won't take the *Tommy Sotomayor approach* and paint a whole group of people one way simply to make a point. Tommy's method is used by taking a drastically negative approach when talking about black people. For example, he'll say something like, "All black women hate their kids" and provide a great rationale exemplifying certain things that some horrible mothers actually do as he's making his point. While this clearly is not true of all black women, Tommy's logic is that, if he said that "some" black women hate their kids, then most black women will say, "Well that's them and not me." At that point they'll be quick to discard the things that he's saying, but if he groups all black women as one then he has everyone's attention and he forces them to actually consider what he's saying. What Mr. Sotomayor does is pretty dangerous and yet, in its own way, it's pretty genius, but that's not my M.O.

I will say this, though, cycles can be perpetuated knowingly and/or unknowingly. Let's examine the commercial radio industry with special attention given to MCs and DJs shall we.

Ask yourself this question: is booty the only conversation that black people are allowed to have on air? Of course not! We have pillars such as Tom Joyner, Steve Harvey, Rickey Smiley, etc. who gracefully use their platforms to bring comedy, current event news, and even special conversations as they pertain to the community. I am grateful for those brothers and many more like them who are not nationally syndicated just yet. These type of shows and conversations, however, are specifically targeted to individuals who are heading to work in the mornings. The demographic of individuals who listen to this type of mature radio are indeed "mature" men and women with an average age of 35 and older. After the morning shows are over, mostly foul lyrics and conversations are played by the DJs and MCs. In Dallas, TX a local radio station does an event called "Twerkin for Turkeys." This is where local residents who would like to receive food for the national Thanksgiving Holiday meet at a central location that the radio station provides and shake their butts in an effort to secure food for their family. Wow. I'll be the first to say that I'm pretty sure that struggling families that arrive and are not willing to degrade themselves in such a manner will still be serviced, but at the same time . . . why lead with that headline though?

Why present our community to the media with this type of standard? Another example is one that happens in every major city in the U.S. Local nightclubs wanting to promote their service pay for advertising on radio stations. They have twerk contests and also big booty contests and advertise this to the individuals listening to the radio. Show off your booty size or booty shaking skills (size because we're living in a time where people are paying heavily to induce the size of their butts), and if you win you can take home anywhere from $500 - $5,000. Hey . . . it's fun right? It's business right? He who has the gold makes the rules right? Yes, but at what cost to the reputation of our community? And I'll say that again continuously—at what cost? Our conversation is more filled with the things that destroy our community rather than the things that uplifts and builds a greater community. Over 90% of the time, we are not the club owners, but we're the club promoters. Over 90% of the time, we are not the media executives, but we are the DJ's and MC's promoting this foolishness. Almost every time, there is a black face used to do the bidding for another race against our own race. We do these things and the world laughs at us. We do these things and then when one of us falls to the ills of systematic oppression then we are quick to vehemently and sometimes violently stand against the oppressor, but have we given our due diligence?

Each individual who identifies as black has to ask this question . . . *am I giving my due diligence?* Entering into the limelight should not mean that one should have to sell his soul for dollar bills. We should not be encouraging our women to dance for money to feed their families, we should not be making light of selling drugs and how it impacts the community, we should not be joking about "hitting licks", robbing hard working people, etc. We should do our due diligence and give our best effort to uplift our brothers and sisters in the best way possible. Now in the case of the radio and other media outlets . . . as stated previously, it's usually a black face who will interface with the people and a white conglomerate (which is getting more diverse by the day) in the decision making executive suite. Again, stepping past racism and looking at it from a money hungry, greed standpoint—we have to see it for what it is and call it what it is. Our first duty as human beings is to know ourselves and to be true to our own selves. No person who is bought by another can afford to be true.

Why am I taking such a strong stand about this? It's because I am tired of seeing violent cycles carried on against black people, and I simply have noticed and identified voids within our culture that need to be patched up. If we can patch these things up then we can witness the liberty and prosperity that we all desire. People of color are rising as the majority in America . . . it's just that we don't own a majority of the wealth. There is no need to topple or overthrow. There is no need to play eye for an eye either as it pertains to discrimination, prejudice, or systematic oppression against those who hold the wealth and have been making the rules. They have been deceiving the masses in an effort to not only rob us of our identity, but to blind us to it through holistic measures. Holistic meaning in many ways, many facets, and through many channels. "Keep poor people poor, keep struggling people struggling, and use the media as a tool to spread hate, racism, and violence throughout urban communities", is their call to service. Money is the only thing that matters to these individuals and they know that their money is threatened if we would simply come up from the trap.

Mass incarceration is ongoing! That's a part of the system, but "Orange is the New Black," right? Hundreds of thousands of black men are being hauled off to prison for drug offenses, but poppin' molly's and selling them is the "in" thing to do though right? Women all across the world are being trafficked, and in our nation women are kidnapped from their families and robbed of their innocence daily, but let's knowingly or unknowingly give drugs to women so they can be our sex toys and call ourselves pimps. Wow . . . what a double standard. There is no way to beautify this. Let's call a spade a spade. When an outsider steps in and kills one of our own we are quick to oppose that outsider, and we should be. Now it's time to deal with the insiders who are similar to crabs in the barrel. There is a way for all of us to experience abundance. There is a way for all of us to experience pure happiness and live in love and peace, and the way we are going is not that way. We have the ability to do this. Hundreds of thousands of our black men and women are being incarcerated and, when they leave the prison walls, they return home to a broken community. They must get a job, but they have a huge stigma—a criminal record. They should pursue higher education—but they cannot get government assistance due to their criminal record. They should live in a safe place, but they cannot even live in government housing projects due to their criminal record. These individuals should have gotten an education while they were younger, but their parents had a similar strain. At some point, they decided education wasn't as important as doing what they could to survive. Even if they have to do things illegally like sell drugs or their bodies... these individuals will even resort to hurting one another to survive if they feel the need to.

This is understood by everyone in the black community, and we all know that this is a part of the systematic plan. So we all know that we have a finger to point outward, but now let's turn it around and point it inward. I dare not take this opportunity to further victimize the individuals among my people who are suffering the most. Too many of us do that and it's disgusting. It is time for those of us who are able bodied to recognize the things that are being held from our people. We must take a stand to resolve this issue and change our condition. That young man or lady who had to abandon their education due to the strain of life . . . who is going back to the community to help him? Who is constructing institutions to combat those things? Who is involved? Are you? The trap is a plan perpetuated by external groups simply to capitalize off of us. Similar to slavery, the price that the victims pay is literally with their lives. This is not for us. We are the head and not the tail. We are the lender and not the borrower. We are highly intelligent and highly capable human beings and we can turn the tide for black people in America.

The Macro trap plan is laid out by parties, external to the race, to perpetuate racial stereotypes, uphold racial biases, and to distract the general population from what really matters. What really matters? Mass incarceration matters, poverty, denial of access to services and institutions, discrimination matters, war, greed, and corruption. So long as we are distracted with everything associated with the trap then our lives will never matter to those individuals. Our families and communities will never matter either. We need financial stability, access to capital, skill building, and cooperative economics. We need to build our own businesses, and rise to the ranks in other established businesses to implement change. None of these things will matter to anyone else if we do not get serious about this matter and as I stated previously: We are paying the price with our lives and the lives of our children.

This is not an easy discussion to have. On one hand we have to identify systematic oppression and call it for what it is. We have to recognize the power that compels our lifestyle. Proper identification is key. After we do that, we then have to look inward at self and see if there are any areas where we can sharpen our own selves in. And this step is the greatest key. This is where we keep ourselves honest, this is where we grow, and this is where we are able to realize the things that we desire most. The black community is represented in every major and minor career field in America—we can rise to the ranks and implement equitable change. We can build our own businesses and have thriving communities. Each member of the black community has a unique spirit and energy given by the Creator of the Universe and this energy has power to create present day realities. We can be the change that we hope to see and we can realize this change and lead happy, prosperous lives. But I believe the first step in attaining that is realizing that external parties have laid out a path for our destruction that we no longer can remain complacent with. Over the next few chapters I'm going to give full, graphic details about how I came up from the trap and built the largest culturally competent publishing firm in the world.

CHAPTER FOUR

A Slave Among Slaves

I don't know the exact circumstances of my birth, but I do know that I was born in Arlington, Texas to two Liberian immigrants named, Louie & Maria McClain. I know that I'm the middle child, I have two sisters who are both close in age, and I can also say my dad wasn't around as much as my sisters and I would have liked during my childhood years. Maybe it was because my parents divorced a little over a year after I was born over religious issues, but shortly after the divorce my dad gathered his belongings and moved to Delaware. I'm not sure why, but that's where he decided to go. While staying in Delaware, he worked at a grocery store called Acme and remained a cashier there until he eventually retired after 20+ years. My father and I are at a good place now, but you'll learn in the chapters to come about our rocky relationship. As far back as I can remember, however, he would come down once a year for a Jewish feast that was held by his church, "World Wide Church Of God", which definitely was Christian cult. Don't get me wrong, his church was Christian, but they believed in keeping a lot of the laws and sacraments of the Old Testament. I'm not sure if they actually killed animals and did the whole nine, but they definitely believed in keeping the feasts. Either way, during his visits, he would spend some time with my sisters and I for about a week and then he would spend the rest of his weekend at the feast. We would spend good quality time together in those short periods. Our days were filled with dressing up and taking family pictures, reading the bible, visiting his friends, and really keeping it simple. There also were rare occasions when my mom, my sisters, and I would take a family vacation to the east coast and we would see my dad and spend time with him. Even though my father wasn't around as often as we hoped for, we did experience good times together when he was present. He also wouldn't hesitate to be strict on us even given the lack of time spent.

I only remember the good times that my father and I had in my younger days, but by the time I turned ten years old . . . I began to notice the discrepancies such as his lack of presence. I also became aware of my mother working 2-3 jobs just to make ends meet and it was around *that* time when my father's lack of presence began to truly have an impact on me. There actually was a time that I didn't see him for a five year period. Before then and possibly even during that five year absence, he would still call every now and then to check on us and ask about our report cards, but ironically, even at that young age—I made it a personal goal of mine to be a greater father than that. I could never imagine being an absent father, so I took an adamant stance against that type of lifestyle.

My mother—she's a queen. She has always worked two or three jobs since I can remember; she's now 64 and she just quit her second job at age 61. This is honestly the very first time I've known her to have only one job. All of her kids graduated college, she has eight grandchildren, she owns land in Africa, she has a home that she rents out here in America, and most importantly—she has a big heart. My mother was able to provide for us financially, but she may have only been to one of my football games as a kid . . . and I played multiple sports as a kid. I knew she couldn't control that part of her life since she worked all the time, but the best part of my day would be when she would come home late at night, as I would come flying down those stairs to embrace her. It was truly the highlight of my days as a child!

The Liberian community was cool in the Dallas, Texas area. Many Liberians left their country to escape an extremely violent civil war that was brewing after a coup in the early 1980's. Many of them migrated to a few major cities in the U.S. with Dallas being one of the major hubs. In the Dallas area at the time, certain Liberian refugees decided to come together to pray for the welfare of their home country and eventually decided to make it a weekly occurrence, so they formed a church. All Liberians who grew up together, went to school together, and even those who were complete strangers—they all found a common bond: unity through spirituality.

Therefore as a kid, I was surrounded by everything African—it was life. When my mother was not working, she loved to be around her Liberian people celebrating their successes with food, gifts, and dancing. Our Liberian church was where I met my best friend Koosh. There were a few leaders at the time, but the late Rev. Nathaniel Johnson Sr., Koosh's father, took charge and led the congregation. Now Koosh and I were about the same age and we would always get in trouble in church. We were always cutting up and laughing at inappropriate times, slapping each other in the back of the head, skipping church and hiding in our hideout spots. Eventually, Koosh's parents moved to my neighborhood which allowed us to walk or ride bikes to each other's house and subsequently caused our friendship to grow even stronger. So, like I mentioned before, practically everything I knew was Liberian for the first few years of my life. My family, my church, and my best friend. The Liberian Community had an organizational body called: *the Liberian Community Association*; which was purely centered on unity among the Liberian diaspora. They would host meetings to discuss the welfare of the country, throw parties, have fashion shows, Liberian Independence Day celebrations, etc. I remember my stepfather would take us to go play basketball every weekend with a group of his Liberian friends. The unity was very strong back then. Today, there are about ten Liberian churches in the Dallas area and some of them have 5-10 regular attendees. Let's just say things just aren't the same as they used to be. I never became conscious of my African identity, though, until I went to elementary school and noticed that I spoke a little differently than the other kids. I was so used to being around my family and attending Liberian weddings, funerals, birthday parties, graduations, and churches that Liberian lifestyle was my norm.

When I entered elementary school, however, I noticed that I was different from most of the other kids and I was actually bullied when my classmates found out I was African. They would make fun of the way I talked and would call me an *African booty scratcher*. That was my initial introduction to public school or an environment not dominated by Liberians. Then when I got into 4th grade, kids began to make fun of me for my hygiene. Constantly spewing out that I had bad breath or that they could smell my arm pits. This was possibly the most embarrassing part of my life—to go to school and have my peers constantly make fun of me, and not know what to do about it! I felt like I was brushing the hell out of my teeth and surely every day I would go home and try harder each time, but every time I went back to school— they would repeat the same things. I remember I used to cry to my mother about the situation and she thought the chocolate milk I drank in the mornings were the cause. After switching over to white milk and still getting made fun of by my peers, I quickly learned that the chocolate milk couldn't have been the cause. I was lost until I learned in a health class in the sixth grade that I was supposed to be brushing my tongue along with my teeth.

Even still, once I learned how to have better hygiene – the kids at school wouldn't let up. The bullying and clowning continued. Even when new kids came to the school, they succumbed to the peer pressure of the more popular crowd and made fun of me. Every time I thought I'd have a clean slate or an opportunity to make a new, genuine friend—it wouldn't happen. Needless to say, these weren't the most fun times of my childhood, but this was something that stuck with me for my entire elementary experience.

I mean, I never got a real haircut from the barbershop until I was in fourth grade! African parents can be so cruel unknowingly, but even so, I was still trying my best to fit in with the crowd. I remember an old friend of mine named Damien Sanders. He would come to school with a fresh bald fade every week and if he missed a weekend of not getting a fresh fade then he would be complaining in school about it. Me on the other hand, I had a fist full of unkempt, nappy hair every day . . . I would just look at him in amazement like bro... YOUR HAIR IS CUT! Maybe fresh fades, appearance, and hygiene wasn't as high on my parent's priority list, but I don't fault them for it. At the time though... I was angry about it as a kid. I wanted to be accepted and I was at a place where I'd do anything to not be bullied. In those times, fourth grade I believe, I began playing football. I played tight end, defensive end, and fullback. Even though I was a rather small guy growing up, defensive end was my favorite position. In my earlier years I played baseball for a while too.

Allow me to rewind for a second, because I left out a very important person. When I was five years old, I met my soon-to-be stepfather "Uncle Chibli". I remember it like it was yesterday. One night he came to our house to take my mom out on a date. The next morning I saw him again in the kitchen making breakfast, and I would see him every day after that. As a kid, I didn't know what a date was, but Uncle Chibli was a very warm and friendly person. He pretty much became the father that I never had. He was a very strict man and even whooped us when my sisters and I were misbehaving, but that was his way of administering discipline and being present. Uncle Chibli could cook very well too! Most of the time, since he pretty much was a stay at home father, he would make us clean up, he would cook for us, and he would help maintain the household. Gender roles weren't a reality growing up in my household.

As a middle child growing up with two sisters, I'd always yearned for a younger brother to talk to, play with, and possibly teach, so I was ecstatic when I learned that Uncle Chibli had three sons including one who was younger than me. By the time I got to 5th grade, Uncle Chibli's sons, Henry, Samir, and Tyrone, came from Liberia to stay with us. Henry was 18 when he came, Samir is 9 months older than me (I was 10 at the time), and Tyrone was 8. Since,

Henry was older and already into adult things, Samir, Tyrone, and I spent the most time playing together back then. Although Samir was taller than me and older by 9 months, we still treated each other like equals, but I still would show him proper respect since he was the older brother. Then there was Tyrone. At first Tyrone and Henry spent a lot of time with each other and we gravitated to different brothers throughout the years, but we all had our times where we favored one over another and spent extensive amounts of time together as we grew older.

When I finally entered middle school in 7th grade, most of my childhood friends split up and went to different middle schools, so I found a whole new circle of friends than the ones I grew up with. I was able to escape the bullying that I was accustomed to in elementary school, and I even got a little popular with the ladies too. However, when I got into 8th grade, I can't recall the exact situation, but one of my classmates from elementary school must have been having a bad day because, when I walked by her vicinity, she made me the laughing stock of school that morning. I was all kinds of "stink breath Louie's" that day during the breakfast hour and, even though it never occurred again after that, the incident conjured up a world of pain within me that I thought was long gone. I went home that day and was like, "Man, I made all this progress and got all these new friends and clout... I really hope they don't start this back up and try to tear me down again."

So as a kid, I was always trying to do what I could to be cool with people and be on their good side. The ironic thing is that, while we were in class, I was friends with most of the kids who would bully me, but it was a different story when that bell rung.

After school, however, I had a completely different experience. I grew up in a suburban area that was filled with what would be considered middle or working class families. My street had a bunch of kids who were relatively my age who I could play with. There was Courtney, Daneisha, Laneisha, JR, Robbie, and a few others who came and went but the ones I mentioned grew up together through our whole grade school experience; we all had a great time. We would play four square, volleyball, hide and seek, tag, truth or dare, and many other fun childhood games. I remember Courtney had a dog named Jewel who, somehow, knew how to jump the fence. Not just any short metal fence, but a tall 7 to 9 foot wooden fence! We would creep up to the fence, antagonize the dog, and then run away to watch it leap up, pull itself over the fence, and then drop down and chase us away. I can imagine all of our neighbors were mad at us because we would jump on the closest car after the self-induced event, but we didn't care. We were just having fun.

So those were a few friends who lived on my street, but off my street and in the neighborhood were Mike Sams, Ced, Garwin, Koosh, Kourtney, Reo, Leo, and a few others. These were my schoolyard friends who we would meet every now and then after school and play together.

******

Every summer my mom would send me and my sisters to Atlanta to be with my favorite uncle—Uncle Big Boy. Now Uncle Big Boy was my favorite guy and he was known for not taking anything from anybody. He would boast and brag about who he beat up, cursed out, and stood up to including the infamous Charles Taylor, the former president of Liberia. Uncle Big boy was like Shaft in my eyes—he never lost a fight! I would visit him every summer for possibly at least ten summers in a row and I loved the experience every time. At times when I felt as if I didn't have a father at home or at all in life, those summers always reminded me that I always had a father in him. He was always there for me. Now, he wasn't the kind of guy who would sit you on his lap and give you wisdom, but he would take you along with him wherever he went and treat you like you mattered. He was a typical African, so he commanded his respect too. You couldn't just say anything to him at any time; you always had to come correct. For instance, if he were to walk up to me and say, "What's up Louie T.?" I would say, "Hello Uncle Big Boy, how are you?" And then we would talk. However, if I was feeling good about myself one day and said to him, "Hey Uncle Big Boy what's up?" He would become angry and tell me that he's not my equal for me to be talking to him like I'm just his friend. Might sound weird, but strangely . . . it's the African way and it's something that I had to learn and accept, and I actually grew to appreciate it with time. But to say the least—he commanded his respect.

I've never seen him verbally disrespect his wife or any woman and my Uncle Big Boy most definitely taught me discipline and the value of family. His wife had about four or five sisters who all lived in the Atlanta area, and they were all very well coordinated. The kids would circulate to each other's houses, we would have picnics and trips to the zoo, we would have major 4th of July celebrations and parties . . . it was fun to be a part of a functional family that actually came together and made family time a priority to say the least. Those were some of my best memories about Atlanta, but those good times ceased when I got into high school.

I'd like to believe that I was always a decent student, especially prior to high school. I earned A's, B's, & C's for the majority of my school years, and I always gave myself a hard time if I thought that I was under achieving. I remember one time during the first day of school, back in elementary, when I entered a classroom and sat down to do my work. I remember getting started and not fully understanding what was happening, but it was the first day of class and my mother was standing outside the classroom door so the pressure was on. Out of impatience and frustration I started pounding my fist against my head and saying to myself, "Come on man, get it together, why can't you understand this?" It took an intervention from my mother to help me gather my composure. Once I got into the 4th grade I was placed in honors classes for a few subjects. Ironically, I didn't realize the switch up until I made it into 5th grade and I started feeling that the classwork was extremely difficult. Well, while it was true that I felt overwhelmed by the content, I also noticed that all of my friends were in other classes and my honors classmates were mainly foreigners and not interested in the jokes I would tell or the cutting up I would do (because I also was a class clown that would get sent to the principal's office over and over again). All of my honors classmates were so studious and, in my young mind, they were too boring. On top of that, I was receiving too many C's, so I convinced my mother that things weren't working out for me and that I needed to get back to my regular classes so I can digest the information better. Somehow she believed me and I returned to regular classes.

The best thing happened to me in 5th grade though .... *Paws!* It was a computer program on the old Macintosh computer that taught me how to type. I remember that old

Mac computer had all kinds of games that helped get kids accustomed to the computer like *Super Munchers, Word Munchers, Number Munchers, Paws,* and a few others. It really made learning fun, and it was on that old device where I realized that I was actually good at something. At that moment in the 5th grade, I knew that when I grew up I would want to work with computers one day. Paws was the best and by the time I was in 6th grade I was typing at over 50 words per minute. It just made me feel good to know that I was good at *something.*

Now as I touched on briefly, middle school was a different experience than elementary days. I was able to make new friends and avoid a majority of the bullies from the past. I made friends with Kenneth, Justin, Michael Magambe, and a lot of lady friends too and on my 13th birthday, I met my best friend Jenne at a skating rink. Well, as kids, we met and immediately became boyfriend and girlfriend for two weeks, and then dated each other's friends, but we remained great friends since then. Kiddy stuff. The best part about that is that Jenne had a friend that she went to school with who would always have "get togethers" at her house. I mean, her mom would allow her to have get togethers and even drive to my neighborhood to pick me up, so it was just great times. The boys and girls would come together with food and we would just talk about things. Small, flirtatious, fun, kiddy talk I guess. Those years were carefree and filled with no true responsibility, and those are some times that most people never get to relive. Needless to say, I greatly enjoyed those years.

In middle school I began to notice gangs, kids getting high, and fights occurred more frequently... gang related fights. I remember a time when a local gang leader came to our school to jump a kid. At first that was such a

scary sight to see, but as I witnessed it over and over again .
. . it sort of became normal. More frightening than schoolhouse
bouts and arguably the scariest thing that ever happened to
me in my life, however, was getting hit by a tornado when I
was in the 8th grade. One day I was in my room watching
The Simpsons after school and the weather man kept
interrupting the show. Every two minutes he would get on
and say "tornado warning" here or "tornado watch" there. At
this age, I didn't know the difference between a tornado
watch and a tornado warning, and I sure as hell didn't
appreciate dude interrupting my evening show at the time
either. After getting tired of the whole ordeal, I decided to
take a nap on my bed. Now, let's see if I can paint a picture
here. I'm on the bottom of my bunk bed and the TV is
directly in front of me on a dresser which is sitting in front
of the window. Next thing I knew, the wind was beating on
my window so violently that it woke me up. When I awoke,
I walked over to the window and looked outside and saw a
Walmart bag floating around in the air and it intrigued me.

For some reason I thought this was like the coolest
sight ever, so I ran to tell my brothers Samir and Tyrone,
who was watching the show with me before I fell asleep, but
now they were in other rooms. Once I grabbed them, we all
went back to my room to look out the window and, as soon
as we made it to the window, we saw a tornado that was
about 50 to 75 yards away. Too close for comfort! As soon
as we were able to turn around and run out of the bedroom
door, about two or three footsteps later, the windows in the
house began shattering. The roof starts coming off, the
doors start flying off the hinges and my brothers and I were
upstairs catching the entire wrath. Actually, the door from
the guest bedroom flew off the hinge and hit my brother
Samir and then we all dropped down to the floor and feared

for our lives. We didn't know if we should try to go downstairs or what to do so we just crawled into the guest bathroom, which was upstairs, held hands, and prayed for God to spare our lives. Once it was all over we went outside to see that our whole street was damaged, people were crying and bleeding, but thank God no one was killed.

Crazy enough, the television that was in my room was gone, and the bed that I was sleeping on was filled with glass from the window. We had a Jacuzzi that was directly outside of my room in the backyard. That Jacuzzi was lifted up by the tornado and thrown over 100 yards away into one of my schoolmate's backyard. I would have certainly been killed had I remained asleep. After a terror filled night like that, we were forced to move out of the house for renovations to say the least.

******

One of the most interesting events that took place when I was a kid was the last day of school. Nothing in elementary school was that exciting (other than lunch, recess, and field day) besides being so happy that summer had finally arrived, but middle school and high school was something a little different. There was always some highly acclaimed fight that everyone anticipated for some reason, and usually of the most treacherous nature. Friends would turn on friends, the bully would get beat up, or some group would fight another group . . . it was just that way for some reason. I vividly remember the day that Big Andrew got jumped. I didn't know what the beef was about; I just knew that big Andrew was the tallest and biggest guy at our middle school. He was in the eighth grade yet possibly weighed about 250 pounds and he was over six feet tall, but he appeared to be a gentle giant. Again, I'm not sure what the beef was about, but I remember walking home with friends and seeing two guys that went to the school wailing away at him. Left – boom! Right – bam! Just back to back blows and I don't recall Big Andrew fighting back, but he wasn't falling down either. Since he was so big, other guys ran to the situation and beat him so badly to where blood started coming out of his mouth and then he finally hit the floor.

This was a scary sight to see, especially since the guys who jumped him were the most feared guys at school. I continued my walk home and then a car pulled up to the group of people that I was with. A guy named Marcus began asking us if we've seen the guys who jumped big Andrew because Andrew's brothers were riding around with baseball bats looking for those guys. Now the leader of the group that jumped Big Andrew was named Leonard and he stayed in my neighborhood. Being that he was the most feared guy around, I thought I could go and lend some assistance and give him a heads up. So, I dropped my last day of school plans to go out of my way to Leonard's house. When I got there, there were about 20 dudes in front of his place who were all hanging out, smoking, and talking about what had just transpired. So I approached the crowd to relay the info that Andrew's brothers were out looking for him and Leonard says, "Ok, hold on for a second." He got on the phone and called Marcus to verify this information and to my great disappointment . . . Marcus denied my claim. Now Marcus just happened to be on speaker phone, so as soon as I heard him call me a liar . . . my heart dropped. It seemed like this whole thing went down in slow motion, but I remember Leonard and the whole crew turning towards me. Leonard's face was so furious that I just took off running in the opposite direction with no shame at all. I had just witnessed what these guys did to Big Andrew and the 20 of them were not about to do that to little old me.

In an attempt to get cool points with the local gang . . . I almost got my own ass whooped. It was an ultimate fail. However, it was at that time that I realized that soon and very soon . . . I needed to become connected with a power source. By that point I had already witnessed what gang activity looked like. Even though I was laying low from the bully situation in my elementary years, I thought to myself – "if this is what it's going to be like in high school then I need to be protected and down with the right people." I then made it my goal to find a way to be down with Leonard and his crew.

By the last day of my 8th grade year, I found myself smoking weed for the first time with the same local gang leader, Prince, who came to my school to jump one of my classmates and who also was Leonard's gang leader as well. It's ironic how life happens. Some of the same people who I was friends with in elementary school turned out to be Prince's neighbors and some others literally were his brothers and sisters. One of my best friends, Ced, lived two houses down from Prince. Ced never had a chance to live any other lifestyle because of this, especially, since he never met his father until after his 30th birthday. Reo and Leo are Prince's adopted brothers who lived with him; they were my friends indeed, but also a ticket into the life of protection and power as well. Later on I also discovered that Prince's half-sister, Ashley, was actually *my* cousin, as her dad and my mother are second cousins. Little by little I was beginning to learn that it's a small world, and my identity was beginning to take shape. I was now plugged in with the gang.

CHAPTER FIVE

Boyhood Days

After middle school, I went to James Bowie High School in my hometown and reunited with a bunch of my friends who ended up going to different middle schools. It was cool because we were used to being on the south side of town, but in high school we had people from all over the city attending Bowie. Now Arlington, Texas, where I'm from, is the second most diverse city in Texas. It's also a melting pot for middle class and upwardly mobile families. If you're below middle class then you can move to Arlington through Section 8 or low income housing and make Arlington your home. All in all, I believe that is a good thing, because everyone should be seeking to live in a new environment, especially one that is free from dire poverty and the negative aspects that are associated with it. The consequence of living in a melting pot is that everyone gets mixed in together, so it's not uncommon to find kids from the hood influencing kids from the suburbs. To the kids in the suburbs, acting "hood" or trying to be hood was a cool thing. We used to watch what it was like to live in the hood on TV through movies like *Boyz In The Hood* and *Menace II*

Society and we would also see it being glamorized in music videos, so this caused us to want a piece of that lifestyle.

Prince, who is originally from Houston, was a gang leader of the Gangster Disciples and he lived on the other side of the main road from me. I can still remember the first day of school; just before lunch, for some unknown reason, Prince had an altercation with someone at the school and a security guard named Fat Mack tried to intervene. Prince ended up assaulting and beating up Fat Mack and got kicked out of school. Based off the time that I spent with Prince in those days . . . I'm pretty sure he never returned to any other school after that, because after school he would either be home or in the streets.

Now that I was in high school, I was able to rekindle my friendship with one of my old friends from elementary school, Tramon Armstrong, may God rest his soul. When we met in 6th grade, Tramon had come from a neighborhood in West Fort Worth (Como) and he was new to the area and he and I became good friends. Tramon had juvenile diabetes and he was a heavy set kid who experienced a lot of complications due to his illness, but that never stopped him from living life as an ordinary kid. Actually, it was Tramon who introduced me to a certain clique.

Even though Tramon was heavy set, he was really good friends with a lot of girls at the school and he also knew how to dance very well. He could dance so good that he was actually a part of this dance clique called "DDK" (Dick'em Down Klick) . . . so you know this group was filled with a bunch of pretty boys. At this point in my life, fighting wasn't the motive; it was more so about dancing, meeting girls, and just having fun. DDK was more of a social status group that competed in dance competitions and won most of them. I, for one, was not a pretty boy and I couldn't dance that good at all, but Tramon said that he could get me in with the clique so I was cool with that. It was truly exciting for me. Here was something I could be involved in that was not completely about power and violence. I remember being like, "Yes!! I'm in . . . I'm with the coolest kids in the city!!" Immediately, I went and got all of my DDK paraphernalia together. I got my embroidered hat and shirt in multiple colors for my wardrobe and everything. The first day I wore my DDK paraphernalia to school, Marcus had suddenly popped up in my life again. Yes, the same Marcus who almost got me beat up by Leonard's crew. He asked me if I was down with DDK and how I got down with the clique. After I told him that Tramon put me on, Marcus told me that he'd get back with me after he spoke with the leaders of the clique.

Next thing I knew, Marcus found me a few days later and told me that the main leader of DDK, named Brandon, said that he didn't know who I was and that when he finds me he's going to beat me up. So I was like . . . WHAT THE HELL? How in the world did I get myself into some mess again? At that point, I went home, threw away all my DDK paraphernalia, and began to prepare myself mentally for whatever was to come next.

At that period in my life I was honestly just doing whatever I could to be accepted. I was trying to have fun and assimilate with whatever my peers said was fun at the time, but my brother Samir was already plugged in with a gang. This was the same gang that Prince led with Leonard as his right hand man and I knew I could get closer to them, but initially I didn't necessarily want to be all the way involved. However, since I encountered a dilemma where some guy I never met was claiming how he was going to inflict pain on me... it caused me to take the next step in my evolution as a young man. And in my opinion (back then), moving on to the big leagues of gang membership was simply *that* next step. Samir and the rest of the leaders were in a grade or two above me, and Prince had already got kicked out of school, so most of the decision making was done by the leadership at the school with my brother right there. So naturally with my own brother being down, my cousin being the sister of the leader, and myself being friends with the leader's brothers and neighbors . . . it was easy for me to slide in.

I was young and I didn't know much about the lifestyle, so I made it my business to become immersed in that life, and eventually, I was able to catch up with Brandon.

One day I was at the mall with my girlfriend at the time and my younger brother. While we were there, my girlfriend spotted Brandon and pointed him out. When I turned toward the direction she pointed in, I saw Brandon standing there with his mother, aunts, sisters, and girl cousins. Everyone knew that he had a big family and that they didn't fight fair *at all*. Actually, they were known to "fight with everything but the kitchen sink". So at the mall, when Brandon and I locked eyes, I made it known to him that I had a problem with him by giving him a cold stare for an extensive period of time. In my mind, he was going to have to show me what he was about and not do all that talking behind my back. Eventually we got into it and exchanged words which continued on until security made us exit the mall. It was a very interesting ordeal. He didn't even know who I was at that moment, but his family didn't care either way. The women were cursing me, pushing me, hitting me with their purses, and then out of the crowd— here comes Brandon running up to steal off on me (punch me). Brandon and I were only able to exchange a few punches before security came and broke up the fight. Unfortunately for me, I was beat over the head and slapped with more purses from the women Brandon was with before security gained full control of the situation.

So there it was!!! I had my claim to fame early on in my high school career. A well-known guy from a rival school stated he had a problem with me, and I took care of business like I was supposed to. I was on a natural high from then on. For the next few years, however, I would continuously run into his friends and cousins and have altercations with them.

******

Gang initiation: Again, since Samir was already down with the folks, I was in too. I started coming around, smoking with them, going to meetings, and then I eventually knew it was official when Prince shook up with me. Shortly after that, so did Leonard and all the rest of the folks. I remember one of the first tests they gave me. I had to beat up a person who used to be my friend a few years back. He was making up his own stories about how he was down with Prince and making other false claims about being affiliated with the gang, so I was sent out to get him and I ended up beating him up in the school gym.

I began learning "lit" (literature) about the founding leaders and their stories: Larry Hoover, David Barksdale, and Shorty Freeman. I learned all about the gang symbols and their secret meanings. I also learned about the violations. They would stress that being a Folk was more like being a part of an organization. If there was a meeting then we had to be there on time or catch violation, and there were meetings during and after school. If you were late then you caught violation. If one of your partners had a conflict with someone and you didn't have their back—you caught violation. If they were getting jumped and you didn't assist—you caught violation. If you were found acting soft or afraid—you caught violation. If your hat was turned to the wrong side—violation; there were so many other ways to catch a violation. Violation meant that you had to place your hands behind your back, and as the gang members surrounded you, you had to get the hell beat out of you and not flinch, fight back, or complain.

I remember when a dude named Tyrone (not my younger brother), who was in a higher grade than most of the members in the gang at the time, had caught violation. No one even told him what was going down, but they notified him that Prince had called a meeting. This meeting just happened to be during school, so everyone rode back to Prince's house during the school day, and unbeknownst to Tyrone . . . he was about to catch violation. This is the same day that one of my friends named Kourtney was able to prove himself. Prince popped off the meeting and notified Tyrone of his error. Kourtney popped off the beating, and after the others beat Tyrone until his both of his eyes were black and his mouth was dripping with blood, they drove Tyrone back to school and told everyone that he was a victim of a rival gang from the other side of town. Imagine that . . . they deceived him into going to the meeting, beat the hell out of him, brought him back to school, and he couldn't do anything but accept his consequences.

Back then our code was to wear baseball gloves in our back pocket. It was the coolest thing in school back then, at least to us, but everyone at school knew what they were for. If there was ever a time where one of us would pull out those gloves, then we all would pull out the gloves and put them on. The next step would be to surround whomever we were opposing at the time and then deliver our street justice.

Looking back on it now, I can't even imagine how I had fun doing those things, but that was life back then. I remember the day of the riot at Bowie. Everyone's normal class schedules were altered due to state-wide testing so everything at school was thrown off. Lunch times were different and people skipped out on class if they didn't have to take the test or if they finished early, but during lunch . . . no one wanted to go back to class after the bell rang. Eventually a fight broke out and a large crowd of 200 – 300 students rushed to a small area to watch it and see what was going on, which led to more chaos. Eventually, the police started chasing numerous kids who were throwing open soda bottles around. This, of course, led to people getting agitated and upset which prompted more fights . . . needless to say utter chaos broke out!

My friend Ced and I happened to be in the mix of the crowd, but we weren't actively involved until a bottle of soda flew my way and hit me. We began to move in the direction of where the bottle came from and I confronted the guy who did it by pushing him. As soon as that happened, a police officer began to mace us and everyone in the area. I can't tell if he intentionally sprayed me, but he definitely got me. That was my first time getting maced, but I washed it off in the bathroom, played it off and proceeded to my next class which was Keyboarding. Now, if you recall, I love computers and at that time I was taking extra keyboarding classes to learn more about it. Keyboarding was the only thing that I knew myself to be good at, so that was the only glimmer of academic hope that I had at the time. I don't really recall the exact situation, but my teacher was a real jerk that day. Now, I might have been a jerk in that time of my life too, but I knew how to be cordial with most of my authority figures. When I got into class, a seemingly small disagreement about tardiness or classwork turned into a nasty attitude from my teacher and I ended up getting sent to the principal's office.

When I got to the principal's office, however, they didn't even want to talk about what happened in class. The principal and staff were actually trying to implement me as a co-conspirator of the riot, which was not true. I played a very small and insignificant part. Either way, they proceeded to kick me out of school and send me to an alternative school. My time at the alternative school was relatively short though… maybe 6 to 9 months. The irony about my life back then was, even though I was involved with trouble and negativity, I still knew how to be an effective communicator and walk the fine line. I always tried to be discreet about the criminal activity that I was in and, according to most teachers, I was a smart kid who didn't cause much trouble. I only had one altercation at the alternative school, in which, I decided to handle those matters after school away from the authorities. That's kind of how I was; I never talked much trash or tried to put myself in positions where I could get caught doing my thing. So, if anyone ever disrespected me openly, I'd simply make arrangements to meet up with them at a central location off school premises so I could beat them up. It was as simple as that!

My parents didn't know the type of things that I was into, and I did all that I could to keep it that way. So there were many times when folks got jumped, beat up, shot at, robbed, etc., but we made sure that we calculated our methods so that we wouldn't get caught.

At this point in my life, I was smoking about three to five times a day. I was drinking 32 and 40 ounce beers and hanging out on the more dangerous sides of town. I was pretty much always in the streets with my friends and my brothers. If we weren't hanging out on the Northside, then we'd be on the Southside at either one of our houses smoking, drinking, and playing dominoes. Girls loved us so we had plenty of them around, and my house was the hangout spot for some time too. I pretty much did whatever I wanted to because my mom was always at work, my step dad was in his room most of the time, and us kids lived upstairs. I came in and left out as I pleased; I snuck girls in and out when I wanted, I had friends sleep over, and I smoked on the roof and the balcony. I just lived a carefree life when I was in high school. My oldest brother Henry was already out of the house. My oldest sister Nikki was away at college, so it was really just Samir, Tyrone, my younger sister Theo, and I. All the boys simply had their way just like I did. Besides that, we practically fought and jumped people every other weekend; we were known for shutting down parties. Whenever we stepped in a place and caught sight of anyone who had ever disrespected us in any way . . . they got the business. No talking needed.

Around that time a lot of the folks started getting their prison sentences too. Prince eventually went away for selling crack, Samir and Leonard went away for aggravated robbery and drive-bys, and some of the older leaders got kicked out of school or moved away. So this is pretty much how things went: as the older leader leaves school, the leadership is passed on to the next grade. After a while, as pertaining to the school scene (which was the major place) Kourtney was given the leadership and I essentially operated as his right hand man. Those times in the streets were interesting because, looking back, everything seems so trivial, but at the moment it just felt so real and like . . . the thing to do. I mean, all the shootings, drive-bys, fights, jumpings, robberies, burglaries weren't even necessary, but to us young and ignorant teenagers - it was life. There was a time when we found a guy who had pulled a gun on my brother Samir before he got locked up. After my friends and I confronted this guy, he proceeded to pull a whole automatic assault rifle out of his trunk. Even though the gun was real, we knew he was bluffing, so he ended up getting smashed less than five minutes later, but I always look back and wonder was it worth all that. The crazy part is, after my friends left that night, I suddenly got jumped by over ten guys simply for wearing blue and that pissed me off because I wasn't even a Crip.

******

Now my first two years of high school was at James Bowie, and my last two were at Juan Seguin High School. Seguin was a newly built school and my junior class was going to be the first graduating class they had. Somehow this solidified my clout even further, as my friends and I were the big dogs of the school and everyone knew who we were. Of course through all this criminal activity, I eventually began selling drugs—weed to be exact. It's interesting how that came to be. When we would hang out on our side of town we would be at either Prince's crib, Kourtney's house, or my house. Kourtney's house was ideal most of the time because his parents smoked and they didn't want him to be in the streets, so they allowed us be there with him and chill out in the garage. We usually would smoke, barbeque, and play dominoes, but one day, during one of our usual games, something changed. Kourtney was sitting backwards in his chair and he suddenly turned the music off. He then placed two backpacks full of marijuana on the table and said, "So what's up, shit just got real . . . y'all niggas ready to get down with this shit or what?" That was my very first time ever seeing that much weed in one place. I was only 16 at the time, but it was an immediate decision. "Hell yeah!! Nigga wassup?" So for the next couple years or so, we added selling weed to our long list of criminal involvement.

We all had our own stash whereby we would have our personal collection *and* enough to sell and make a profit for the re-up. And we had clientele! Back then we were the guys on the Southside. Everyone knew that we would whoop some ass, they knew we were cool as hell, and they knew that we always had some green. All the while, I'm still making ABC honor roll, but I'm also getting kicked out of classes for my class clown behavior too. Getting kicked out of class often landed me in in-school suspension (ISS) where I actually met my first mentor – Craig Cole, the ISS teacher. He did what he could to reach me then, even though I initially didn't care to see it. I actually attempted to fight him the first time we met after he looked at me, smirked, and said, "I thought sagging was left back in the early 90's." I mean mugged the shit out of him, but I couldn't do anything because he was a teacher, and I wasn't that stupid. But Mr. Cole or Craig would take me out of the class to talk to me when he seen me struggling or having a bad day. Every time he pulled me out of class he tried to speak some sense into my head and, at that point of my life, he was the only person whose actions showed that he believed in me. He would plant many seeds in my head, and tell me about how his life was and how he made similar mistakes back in the day.

One argument that he would use that I didn't heed then, and I still think it's not a good argument to use is — *You shouldn't be doing this kind of behavior because you're from Arlington (the suburbs).* The fallacy with that type of thinking is that, in the mind of a kid at least, it doesn't matter where you're from. If a kid is seeing deviant behavior getting rewarded then he/she will seek to be involved in that deviant behavior. Period. If selling drugs looks cool, fighting, shooting, having sex, and all that stuff—kids will do it regardless of their background. This is why it's important to have a strong family background, with a father, and a community of mentors, but that's not always the case . . . even in the suburbs. All kids are thinking about is pride, recognition, power, and how they cannot be the butt of the joke. Either way, Craig would go above and beyond to reach me with positivity and he even would call and check up on me from time to time. There was a time when I was about to run away from home and he happened to call me that day, so I told him what I was about to do. This gentleman proceeded to come to my house, pick me up, and he ended up talking me out of it. Craig actually took me on a road trip for the weekend since he was traveling four hours away to visit his fiancé.

When we arrived in Midland, Texas I was astonished. His soon-to-be father-in-law, who was a Caucasian man, had a real estate company that built the nicest custom made mansions and houses. And up until that time . . . I had never seen anything so magnificent. I mean, my mind was blown. I saw a new side of life. Here it is, all I'm doing is everything to destroy my own life and others, meanwhile, people are in different places of the world living beautiful lives in beautiful environments. I felt so small and embarrassed at that time, but in a good way. Up until then, I honestly never witnessed that much beauty and peace. I realized that life could be lived in a completely different way, and that life didn't have to be what I was making it out to be. I am forever indebted to Craig Cole for being there for me, investing in me, and planting the seeds which ultimately changed my life, even though the change happened many years later.

When I came back home to the gang . . . it was the same old thing. Now, as I mentioned previously, the group that I was a part of was the Gangster Disciples. There weren't many GD's in the area where I was, but every now and then we'd meet Vice Lords or Folks from different parts of the country. One folk from Mississippi was named B.T. He started going to Seguin my senior year and let us know that we claimed the same thing, so automatically . . . we did a brief interrogation to confirm knowledge and then accepted it. I say accepted it, because B.T. wasn't tough. One day, it came to our attention that B.T. was into it with some new kids who just started going to Seguin and weren't aware of our reputation. So I sent a message for these guys to meet us at the park to settle the situation. When we got to the park, there were a lot of people there including both of the new guys. I asked if they were trying to jump B.T., and they denied it and said that only one guy wanted to fight him. Since that was the case, I said "ok cool . . . y'all go ahead and do what you gotta do." Immediately I noticed that BT was all kinds of scared!! He was shaking; he didn't know how to post up, nothing. So at that time, I knew that I couldn't allow this to go down like that so I stopped it before it went any further. I put my hand on BT's chest and told him to step back and I proceeded to take off my hoodie. I fought the dude, won, and went on about my way.

Shortly after that, rumor made its way around to me that the guy who I recently beat up had a cousin that was supposedly looking for me. I was appalled! Looking for me? I wasn't hard to find . . . I mean I did go to two schools and had two or three jobs, but I was always available when there was a party. And folks knew where I hung out at, but I kept hearing these rumors for a couple weeks until I had enough. So one weekend, I got strapped up and actively went looking for these guys. I had my gun, extra bullets, and a plan to lure these guys into a certain alley way, hop out the car, and kill them. This was a crazy weekend, because on Friday, Saturday, and Sunday . . . we ran into three separate groups of people that we already had issues with - every night - and I attempted to kill each one of them each night. The main night was Saturday when I saw the guy who supposedly was looking for me. As soon my friends and I pulled up to the party, he and his friends pulled up to the party and it was on sight right then and there until security broke up our altercation and told us to leave. So, as was my M.O., I told him to meet me at the park.

We pull up to the park and both groups are four or five deep each, so I gave one of my boys my gun while I fought. As I'm fighting one guy, my boy Mike Sams is fighting another guy, and others were standing by watching. While this is going on, my friend who was holding my gun gets sucker punched by one of the other guys who were there. Granted, we knew these guys! Hell, we were even friends at a certain time years back, so my boy totally didn't see this coming. Well, he gets sucker punched and essentially knocked out cold. When he hit the floor . . . my gun slides out to the ground. Everyone stopped fighting at that time and the other group of guys started rushing towards their car . . . but it was too late for them. I ran to the gun, picked it up, and started firing off in their direction and luckily for me . . . no one got hit. That is how the night begun. By the time the night was over, we had already conducted two drive-bys and a stake out of one of the dude's house. We were even calling their home phones trying to trick them into coming outside so we could kill them. I was totally out of my mind and I would say more, but I'm not sure of the statute of limitations at this time.

When Monday came back around, my friends and I went to school, but the other guys we had a problem with did not. People who knew about everything that went down were staring at us in amazement saying, "I can't believe y'all showed up to school." Our response was, "Man . . . where them niggas at?" We received reports that they were hiding at hotels, that we shot up the wrong bedroom (one of their baby sister's room), etc. . . . it was bad, but we didn't care. Later on that day, however, the tables turned. Now it was I who was receiving phone calls telling me to come outside. I looked out the window and I saw guys creeping in cars (driving slow down the street) waiting on me. So at that time . . . I figured that enough was enough . . . I had to tell my mother what I was into. All of the OG's were in jail or prison and I knew that I didn't want to be there or dead, which were my only two options at that time. I had to go ahead and take that L. Now, the only time when my mother had a clue of the things that I was involved with was a time when I decided to handle business at school. It came to my attention that some guy had my name in his mouth. When I got the news, I was so infuriated, mainly because dude was wack. So I walked right up to him, punched him in the face, threw up some gang signs, and smooth walked away. I would have been *Scott Free*, but he told on me and then there was a whole meeting with the police, principals, and both of our parents with video footage of the entire altercation. Sadly enough for me, I didn't know about the video footage, so of course I lied about it. Usually my mother wouldn't believe a thing that I said, as she would always take the teacher's side, but this time . . . she fell for the okie-doke and vehemently defended me. After the tape was revealed . . . my heart dropped and she lost all confidence in me. I broke her heart.

So at the news of my crazed out weekend, she placed me on the first flight out of the state that very same night! I was on my way to live with someone who I never really new that well – my father.

******

In Delaware I was in a totally new environment, as my mom sent me to live with my dad who lived with his wife and my half-brother. Now the good thing about moving away was that Texas schools required two years of foreign language, and I had barely made it past the first year of Spanish (I definitely took Spanish 1 three times), but in Delaware I only needed one year to be able to graduate. So I was good. I was able to sign up for more electives to take, because their whole school structure was different from ours back home. I took criminal justice and history classes where I learned about Malcolm X and the Nation of Islam—which I never knew anything about.

In Texas I always had a job and ways to get money so, even though I was in Delaware, I still wanted to do the same things especially since I was no longer getting free lunch like I did in Texas. There were a few days that my dad's wife would take me out to go look for jobs. Actually, she did that for about a week. I filled out many applications, and when Pizza Hut called me for an interview—I told my dad out of excitement. Here was his response to that, "When did you ask for my permission to get a job?" Aw man, I was astonished. Here's a guy who wasn't paying child support, here's a kid who's been working since he was 15, and I'm in a whole new state trying to be productive . . . AND THAT WAS HIS RESPONSE! I was like, *oh hell naw man*. So I had to tell him, "Yo . . . I been doing this man. I'm 18 years old now and you're telling me that I have to ask you for permission to get a job....?" Remember, I haven't even seen dude in like five years and he wasn't there to raise me or help me learn to be a man. He couldn't protect me from entering a gang or anything that spawned from it . . . but he wanted me to ask for his permission to do what a man should be doing..? Naw bruh.

That wasn't the end of it either. He told his wife not to help me anymore so, when I got hired at Pizza Hut, I had to walk to and from work in the snow for about two miles each way until I learned how the bus system worked. But yeah . . . that still wasn't it; my dad wanted me to be with him when he cooked. He tried to show me how to "white glove" clean the house, and he was trying to instruct me in the proper ways of hygiene . . . like - he was telling me about putting powder under my arms after I bathed at night and things. In my head I'm like "bro . . . I've already mastered these things. Where were you at when I was 5, 6, and 7 years old getting bullied at school though?" By now you can obviously tell that things were very awkward between us. I was only supposed to live with him for six months until I graduated, but that got cut short in half the time. There were really three reasons why we got into it. The job situation was one. Then, when Valentine's Day came around, my mother sent me money (this was right before I began working at Pizza Hut). She sent it via USPS in a Valentine's Day card made out to Louie McClain. No one was home when the postal worker arrived, so they left a slip for someone to retrieve the package from the post office. I decided to ask my step mother about my mail after a few days of not hearing anything about the package, and she told me about the slip and said that my dad had it. Yet, my dad refused to give me the slip because he said, "the mail is in my name, so I'll go get it when I'm ready." I let him slide even though I knew the package was for me! After two weeks of dealing with this situation and not getting what's rightfully mine, I decided to approach my dad about it for the final time.

I walked up to him while he was feeding his four year old son and I asked him about it. His response was, "Can't you see that I'm feeding my son." As you can guess, I immediately became furious! I told him that I wasn't going to get out of his face until he gave me what was mine. He tried to walk around me, but we eventually made it to the point where my back was to the stairs and I wasn't allowing him to go down. I then said to him, "If you push me down these stairs, you will see what I will do to you." At that time, his wife called the police and they tried to get me locked up for making threats. When the police arrived, they inquired about the situation and I told them that he had been withholding mail from me. The police then told him that it is a federal offense to withhold mail, and then that's when my dad did the unthinkable. He asked the police what he needed to do to get me out of the house. The response: *provide your son a 30-day notice.*

From that day forward I began walking on pins and needles. I mean, sheesh, I already was running away from a life in prison or death, and now my own father is trying to make me homeless in a strange land. I told my mother and she spoke with him and tried to get people to talk him out of it and, for a moment, I thought he would have a heart. He told my mother that he would allow me to stay. A few days later, when I came home from school, my step mother told me that I had mail and that she wanted to take me to the post office. When we got to the post office, I receive a certified envelope that said from Louie McClain at my dad's address to Louie McClain at the same address. My dad wrote me a whole B.S. letter and ensured that it was certified stamped to provide me with 30 days to get out of his house. After much anxiety and toil, my mother was actually able to find some friendly Liberians who lived nearby in Delaware that would take me in. I graduated from William Penn High School in Delaware and my dad never showed up, but my Uncle Big Boy, Uncle Chibli, my mother, and my sisters showed up though and that was all that I needed.

When I came back to Texas for the summer, the only thing that was on my mind was laying low, so I could leave again for college. I had already gotten accepted to Pensacola Christian College, but I really didn't care. All I ever wanted to do back then was get a job at a factory, and live in an apartment while supporting my family. As long as I could sustain a living doing that . . . I figured that I'd be cool. Of course, my mind changed drastically once I learned the way the world works with economics, gentrification, and the need for generational wealth; but that's just where my mind was back then. Before I went to school I did see a few of the guys who I was initially beefing with before I left for Delaware, but there was no issue. Actually, one of the guys who I was beefing with had actually shot a guy a few weeks after I left for Delaware the previous year and was already shipped off to prison.

I just spent my time preparing myself mentally for college, because I had recently learned that the school I'd be going to was extremely strict and people get kicked out of there often. I didn't want to let my mother down again and I knew that the college was unaccredited, but I really only agreed to attend because I knew that it was cheap enough for me to work and pay off half of the bill. I just had ignorant pride like that to say the least.

Regarding the rules of the school, here are a few: You can't touch girls in any way . . . not even shake their hand, lights out is at 11PM, a tie must be worn every day, a suit and tie must be worn to dinner, no gum chewing in school buildings, if you're late to class you get demerits, if you don't show up to class you get demerits, if your bed is not made you get demerits, if you go to the movies you'll get kicked out, if you have music with drums you get 10 demerits for each song, and if you get 150 demerits you get kicked out. It was a bunch of ridiculous rules!!! I mean . . . I have a friend who got kicked out for speaking in tongues. So even though I was taking time to mentally prepare myself for school . . . I gave myself three weeks. Surely I'll be kicked out of PCC within the first three weeks . . . boy was I wrong.

CHAPTER SIX

The Struggle For An Education

W elcome to Pensacola Christian College (PCC). Actually, the night before I went to PCC, my younger brother Tyrone and I had our last smoke session in the car, and the next morning my mom and Uncle Chibli drove me to Florida where my school was located. When we arrived, we made it to the hotel my parents were going to be at, and after that we headed straight to the chapel. I remember entering the auditorium that day and being in culture shock—I had never been around so many white people at the same time in my entire life! The capacity was about 5,000 graduate & undergrad students along with alumni who attended the church and a few locals as well. The black population appeared to be less than 10% and Asians and Latinos were about 10% as well. It was astonishing and I was standing in awe. We went to the café after the service and I remember seeing a bunch of people dressed in church clothes. I remember standing there in utter disbelief thinking about the lifestyle I was accustomed to and recalling the school rules they had; I just knew I wasn't going to make it. At that time I heard my mother's voice, "Louie T.", she said in a very concerned voice. I turned to look at her as she patted me on my back and said, "You'll do fine". By this time she already knew all the trouble I was capable of, but she still believed in me.

Again, Arlington, Texas, where I'm from, is the second most diverse city in Texas. Come to my city anytime of the year and you'll see black folks, Mexicans, Asians, and white people everywhere. I personally don't recall experiencing racism, especially as a child, because it either wasn't there or everything just went over my head. At PCC, however, I was now surrounded by white people who were from different walks of life; cultures and lifestyles that I wasn't accustomed to. For instance, I've never been around so many people who came from a farm or who sport confederate flags on their belts. The black crowd was interesting as well. I'm saying black here because there were many Africans, Haitians, Bahamians, and many other black people from different parts of the world including Papau New Gunea. Nonetheless, my experience back then was that a lot of the black people at the school were like the guys from the movie *Get Out*, seemingly brainwashed with a desire only to assimilate into the dominant culture. Seriously, it was as if some of my brothers there were under some sort of spell, because they weren't cultured and many of them even walked and talked differently. It appeared to be a little more than *mere* assimilation. They almost wanted the exact identity of being white. But of course that wasn't all of the black people there . . . just a moderate percentage. The Africans and Caribbean residents potentially had the strongest base at the school though. They stuck together, studied with each other, and had their own historical, unity events . . . including playing Fifa World Cup!!

I remember Adam and JJ's group of friends. Now these were a part of the strongest "Black American" preacher groups on campus. Notice my full distinction here (Black American preacher group). Their practice would be closest to black Baptist churches, but more fundamental in their methodology. The school church was predominantly white and they considered themselves "Independent, Fundamental Baptists", but then you had a few black Pentecostals that attended the school too. The thing about PCC is that it was very discriminative *even* against fellow Christians. You couldn't speak in tongues, they believed only in the King James Version of the Bible, you couldn't listen to Kirk Franklin or any modern gospel music that had drums, and the list went on and on. It was like our free will was somehow trapped in a prison.

As you can see, the rules at PCC were very strict and all I could think to myself was, "*WOW!* This institution really has the audacity to tell us that we can't touch girls, watch movies, and listen to music with drums in it. I mean what the hell were they trying to run here, a Buddhist Monk monastery?" And to add to the list of DONT's: we weren't allowed to be off campus with a girl even if it was just to walk across the street to get ice cream at McDonalds. You actually had to sign out, and tell the school exactly where you were going and when you'd be back. If you made a pit stop anywhere else you could be kicked out for being 'deceitful'. You couldn't go to the movies or you'd be kicked out. During a certain part of the day you could walk and talk with the opposite sex outside, but not in certain areas after the sun begins to set. Each room in the dorms had a maximum of three to four roommates and the dorms had two floor leaders for each floor who were usually ministerial majors. Their job was to monitor and regulate the activities on the floor including lights out, behavior, and daily room inspections. The room had to be thoroughly cleaned each morning and if anything was found to be not in order then you'd get demerits. The floor leaders would also ensure we weren't studying after lights out, as they would check on us and report accordingly within their chain of command.

During my first two years at PCC, I was rooming with floor leaders and my first job was at *Abeka Book*, the school's homeschool initiative, as a Customer Service Representative. The next thing I did was work in Maintenance and my first job there was being the Garbage Man. I eventually moved over to other duties within maintenance, and my last job at the school was as a Security Guard. Prayer groups were an interesting time and very special to me though. We would have prayer groups every night for 15 minutes with exception to Sundays and Wednesdays since we had an evening church service on those days. Of course with my background, I knew nothing about adequately communicating with God and I didn't even know if I wanted to when I first began school at PCC. However, prayer group is where I met my Spiritual Father, Paul Achaempong, who also went on to become one of my best friends in college.

In prayer groups early on, everyone there would always ask me if I had anything to say or if I wanted to pray or if I had a prayer request. My answer was the same each time—no. A part of me was shy, another part didn't know how to pray, and then another part just didn't want to. The interesting thing about it is that my peers never judged me in those times. They were patient, encouraging, and gave me a pass week after week. After a while they were like, "Louie .

. . just open your mouth and say things." "Just talk to God", they would say. And it came a lot easier than I expected; I was able to open up and pray.

******

I didn't know much about anything academically when I first got to the school, but I did what I had to do to make my way. I was accustomed to being an ABC student and I tried to keep the same study habits that I had while in high school, but the schoolwork was so overwhelming. I wasn't accustomed to loads of work, so I knew I had to do something different to make good grades. I tried studying after school in my room, but having so many roommates led to too many distractions. My roommates didn't have a problem with the distractions, but I found out very soon that I needed to be in solitude to get good work done. Shortly after that, however, I began hanging out with JB and Gabriel, my friends from the Bahamas, and I began to follow their lead when it came to studying. Every day after dinner they would go to the library, open their bible, read for 30 minutes to over an hour, and then they would open their class books. I was in shock! Here I am dreading to study and wanting to hurry up and get it over with, but here they are jump starting their study session with an hour's worth of unrelated content! The funny thing about it is that if anyone began talking at the table in the library, these gentlemen would politely get up from the table and move to a solo desk cubicle so they could continue to focus. So I simply adopted their practice. Somedays I would wake up around 4 AM to get ready for class and then go to work after that or I would wake up at 4 AM and go to work and then head to class.

Either way, I'd end up having dinner with my friends and head directly to the library.

Interesting enough, I started taking initiative to be more focused about my studies. Even after my long days . . . I began following JB and Gabe, because they taught me how to be studious and serious about my school work. I remember how things were when I first started taking classes. I would sit in the back of the room and position myself behind a classmate to simulate reading or studying, but I'd actually be sleeping. Ironically, I never got called out in class, but there were a few times where I was definitely snoring and drooling. My classmates were sure to call that out! But after a few weeks I made it my business to sit in the front of the class. I started raising my hand if I had questions and I began to force myself to pay attention. Later on, I started finding great interest in the classes and my favorite class was Criminology – the study of why people commit crimes. Actually, learning the theories of Classicism and Positivism might have been the beginning of my intellectual journey.

Classism is the argument that everyone has a free will and that people commit a crime because they made a conscious decision to do something wrong, so they should receive punishment for their behavior. Positivism, on the other hand, says there's a strong determining factor as to why people commit crimes and they wouldn't exhibit such behavior if they weren't placed in certain situations. It's the notion that if someone is in dire poverty and they're hungry—then they'll steal. If they come from a bad environment then they'll be products of their environment, etc. With my background of criminal activity, this was very interesting to me because it spoke directly to my experiences and made me think about myself, my friends, and other people who had similar influences as I had in the past. I was a criminal, all of my friends did terrible things, and the music we listened to and people we were around constantly promoted bad things. Don't get me wrong, I was born in the suburbs and became influenced, but my friends were born in inner cities and just happened to live near me.

So I started asking myself: Where do I fit in with these theories? How does it relate to my friends and others involved in the system? What does this mean for the young brothers out there in the world still in those environments? I felt like Positivism was talking directly to me and my demographic.

As I began finding interest in my classes, I eventually made the Dean's List. That was the first major academic feat I ever had and I made the accomplishment during my first semester too. My mother was so proud that she submitted it to the local newspaper in Arlington! Now, I chose Criminal Justice as my major because I happened to take a class when I was in Delaware and I really enjoyed it. I also didn't know what I was good at before heading to college, so I took up criminal justice because it was familiar. At first, I thought it might be an interesting occupation to be a detective, but after I learned that doing so would call for two or more initial years as a street cop, I decided to not to pursue that direction.

In class there were opportunities to go to the nearby grade school and direct traffic a few mornings out the week for extra class credits, so I knew I needed to take advantage of that. I had the whole uniform and whistle, and learned how to make the right hand signals and gestures.

There was the one incident which ultimately determined the direction of my life from then on out. One morning as I was directing traffic, a frantic woman pulled up to me and told me about a kid who was stranded in the middle of a busy road intersection. I immediately left my post and ran to the street to only find a five year old kid crossing the street by himself. I rushed to his aid and held his hand and assisted him in getting to school. Even though the occurrence may sound like a trivial event, it was at that moment that I understood my purpose in life. I remember seeing so much innocence in that child that it made me think about my past. It was at that exact moment when I knew in my heart that I wanted to do something to ensure the purity of kids and to help them get on the right path.

My life prior to PCC had caused me to face death on a few occasions. I had been robbed at gunpoint, shot at, a victim of a drive by shooting, stabbed, jumped by over a dozen guys, and my house had even been hit by a tornado when I was in the eighth grade. As if all that wasn't enough, Hurricane Ivan was on a course headed directly for PCC a mere three weeks into my college experience after I was already changing my life for the better. Ivan was a couple hurricanes before Hurricane Katrina which swept New Orleans clean back in 2005, but all I knew is that I was fed up with near death experiences and natural disasters at that point. Everyone was panicking, driving back home, and my school actually shut down for a few weeks, but I didn't have a car or a way home at that time. The school had designated shelter buildings, so I just went where I was told which was the Sports Center where kids were playing board games, bowling, racket ball, and praying. I found a quiet corner to fall asleep in as soon as I entered the building and, when I woke up, Hurricane Ivan had already came, did its damage to the city, and moved on. We didn't have classes for a couple more weeks and it was an interesting time because a lot of the facilities were inoperable, but we made due the best we could. I remember meeting Tammy around that time.

Tammy was a really good girl; she actually was JB's younger sister and she also had a boyfriend back home in the Bahamas. I also was in a relationship with my girlfriend in Texas, so the whole ordeal was interesting in the beginning. We would meet up for lunch and dinner with her brother and friends, get in the Word, and have interesting conversations about all types of things. I initially would sit and listen as the group conversations went on, ensuring that I didn't open my mouth foolishly and say something I wasn't all too familiar with. Tammy and I were always together for the first three years of college, but we never made anything official. When we were together at school nothing else mattered and the relationships that we had back home faded away each day that Tammy and I grew closer through the Word. There was some back and forth with Tammy and her boyfriend, and eventually they got engaged during the time she went back home to the Bahamas, but both of us eventually broke up our stagnant relationships back home and fell in love with each other.

Boy was JB excited about that!! I was sort of surprised because I was the only person at the school who knew about my horrible past, but now that my life was going in an opposite direction . . . people were really digging my mental and spiritual growth.

A lot of things transpired within the first month of school; the most important thing of all was getting saved. One day after class, while checking my mailbox, I spotted my friend JJ checking his mail. Now JJ was a black guy, who was of Haitian descent, but I couldn't tell the difference . . . he appeared to have the same rough edges I had. As he and

I struck up a conversation, we ended up walking back to his dorm and, once I entered in his room, I saw his roommate Adam. Adam was reading the bible and out of the blue he closed the bible and asked me, "Louie, if you died today, would you go to heaven or hell?" I pretty much blew off the question and just laughed a little and said, "I really don't know if I even care to believe in that stuff." I brought up reincarnation and everything else people say when they don't know about the gospel. Adam paused and just stared at me, but when I was done talking, he pointed his finger at my face and said, "Louie . . . you are a fool." He then attempted to show me where the bible says, "The fool has said in his heart that there is no God," but I wasn't trying to hear it. All I knew was that this nerdy ass looking dude with glasses just pointed in my face and called me a fool. I wasn't having it. So he and I started exchanging words and I even started cursing at him telling him how I'd whoop his ass. Adam then started pounding his fists and said, "Louie . . . I will throw you into this wall!" And the two of us were about to go ahead and get to it until JJ came and stood in between us. He stopped the arguing and pulled us closely and said, "You see man . . . this is it. This is the exact reason why we need to be saved. No one is perfect and we've all sinned. Adam is saying these things not because he thinks he's perfect or better than you . . . he's saying this because he has a sinful nature too. For all have sinned and fell short of the glory of God." As JJ carried on with that tone, all of a sudden I forgot that I was just about to knock Adam's head off and get kicked out of school. The next thing I knew I was on my knees praying the salvation prayer and surrendering my life to Jesus Christ.

Concerning JJ and crew, you could tell that he and some of the people in his circle had a negative past just as I did. Now, I know that some of them were second semester or second year at that time, so I'm not sure how long they had been doing the Christian walk, but one thing I knew for sure was that I wasn't too far removed from the street life. Hell, I was only at the school for two or three weeks at that time! JJ's crew had turned their life around and got saved, but they still had their rough edges. All their messages were hell, fire and brimstone! They would call people out, point their fingers, and enjoy controversy for the gospel's sake. That's just how they operated. They also agreed with the school about anti-Pentecostalism.

Paul and JB were of a different Christian vibe though. They were more non-denominational, yet closer to a Pentecostal vibe. They operated in the Word, but also had a great deal of emotional availability to God too. They were into speaking in tongues, lifting your hands in church (which was shunned at PCC), laying prostate, and crying out (I mean ugly face crying each Sunday) type worship. But you could tell that they certainly had an intimate relationship with God. Paul could get me into the word with ease. In bible class we had to read four to six chapters a week and memorize things, but Paul would open up one chapter and focus on only a few verses and expound on them with ease. That is when I first began to deep dive and dissect the Word of God and gain an understanding. This is the type of crew who would instruct me to spend hours and possibly days fasting and praying in the prayer room on our dorm floor. And I was trying to do it all: hear God's voice, fast, pray for over 24 hours, and wait for the Holy Spirit to descend on me so I can speak in tongues.

Paul and JB were my go to group of friends, but when I got saved, JJ's crew approached me about getting baptized. They showed me the Ethiopian eunuch scripture about how baptism was the next step in the Christian faith after getting saved. I signed up for baptism at the campus church, but then the church postponed the next baptism to a date that was a few months out. So these guys compelled me to sneak into the campus pool with them after hours and get baptized, which I did.

The Campus Church was an independent, fundamental Baptist. They started on time, finished on time, and you had to dress up to go to church. They were very strict and not liberal at all. The messages were mainly expositional with exception to a few topical exhortations, but needless to say . . . I got a holistic view of Christianity during my time at PCC. We had bible class twice a week, chapel Monday-Friday essentially, prayer group five days a week, church three times a week, and I even participated in "Christian service". I would go downtown and witness to people on the street. There were many types of Christian services, but I preferred approaching random strangers downtown. I remember those times vividly because we all would be so excited when we would bring back our reports. After church on Sunday and Wednesday nights we would go to the top of the stairs on the dorms and we would meet up to pray and preach. About 20-30 guys would meet up on the top of the stairs and be seated. Then one person would stand up, pray, and sit down. Next, a guy would stand up and give a 5-10 minute devotional, sharing what he has learned and when he would sit down then the next guy would do the same. We would do this until we had about 10-15 minutes left until lights out and then we'd run back to our dorms. Those were very fun times for me.

My main crew was with Paul, JB, Gabe, Tammy and Toya (Tammy's friend), eventually O'Neil and Thad joined the group as well. Basically, everyone was from the Bahamas besides Paul and I and even though Tammy and I "dated", we never attempted to do anything that would jeopardize our status at the school and more importantly . . . our relationship with God. Regarding our status at school, we couldn't even touch girls. If we touched girls in any type of way—even if it's not malicious sexual touching, then we could get "socialed" which meant that you literally couldn't communicate with the opposite sex for the next 2-3 weeks. Floor leaders and school officials would have your name on a list and they'd be watching out for your violation because if you did . . . then you'd get kicked out. But there were things we could do on campus like hangout at the sport center, chat at the commons building, and dining. As stated previously, Paul was my spiritual father and I remained close to him because he was a good friend, but he also had mature guidance, wisdom, and the Word. If I was feeling some type of way he would always have a scripture for it. He took me under his wing and guided me. African men who are in the Word have very strong and dynamic personalities, and Paul was nothing short of powerful. Even though Paul and JB were my two closest relationships on campus . . . our close knit friendships eventually fell off in time.

Tammy and I were pretty much courting each other and marriage was the ultimate next step, but later on things changed when Paul started calling out things that were "carnal" about Tammy and it started making me look at her a certain way. Ignorantly, I started to judge her and her walk with God. Tammy and I were supposed to be preparing ourselves to change the world for Christ, and the things that Paul was telling me began making me second guess her commitment. I was probably a total jerk about this, but after a failed attempt of addressing it with Tammy, we decided to go our separate ways. As life would have it, a few weeks later, there was Tammy in the café dining with another guy who had an interest in her. By the next year, they were engaged and I learned a very valuable lesson—always follow your heart.

In the process of time, Paul and I began having disagreements and we both eventually found other groups of friends to spend our time with.

******

I knew that I wanted to work with juveniles, so I started mapping out how my life would go. The first thing I did was begin working with Campus Security to build my resume. Now, one could only get in the security field through recommendations, so a guy that I looked up to in my major, Delano James, plugged me in with his boss since he was already in the job himself. After a while I got my internship with the Florida Department of Juvenile Justice (FDJJ) and then I eventually began volunteering with their probation department. During my time volunteering, I noticed that kids could get their probation violated by doing the smallest things such as: being kicked out of class, not passing class, skipping school, not going to detention (school detention), etc. There were so many restrictions on them (negative motivation), but there wasn't much positive motivation to actually help them be successful in their endeavors of doing well at school and successfully completing probation. At that time, I rounded up a group of my classmates and we took the initiative to make tutoring a court ordered sanction. I visited courthouses, spoke with judges and probation officers, created a survey for probation officers, posted flyers about our initiative in detention centers, and many more. I simply identified a void. I saw that the federal government gives money to schools to have tutoring services in low income areas and I was able to demonstrate that the resources were readily available, so not much needed to be done but for the judge to mandate it. We did find a small pocket of success with that initiative and eventually after I graduated I got hired at the detention center.

My tutoring initiative was this - kids could violate their probation for practically anything and go back to jail or juvenile prison. My thoughts were, if they could miss school and get a violation or if they could not pass their classes and be violated, it only makes sense to mandate tutoring since everything else is being mandated. At least this way kids would be in the best position to gain an understanding and be more apt to gain an interest in schoolwork, and possibly even stay away from the street. I rounded up a few friends from class and we would have meetings in the school library to map out my vision. I conducted research about Title I Schools and how low income neighborhoods have federal funding for tutoring. I found out where those neighborhoods and community services were and how we could use all of the information to our advantage. One of my team members created a flyer (a graphic design major) and I began making my routes to probation offices and court houses throughout the county. It was very interesting to see the court officials who liked the idea and the ones who opposed it. I was surprised to find African-Americans who opposed it, but to each his own. It was a bit discouraging, but at the end of the day, I was able to see judges put this practice into effect in Escambia County, Florida and a few probation supervisors encouraged their team to look into these services as well. I was successful!

******

Sometime during my first year at the school, I remember going to one of the school deans (Dean Oman) and asking about having a black history month celebration. He declined by stating "There isn't a white history month." That statement pretty much sums up PCC; draw your own conclusions. I recall the night of an incident that had me shook for a bit. As usual, lights out is at 11pm, but my roommates and I didn't always go straight to sleep some nights. Sometimes the floor leaders would do two checks and other times they would do one, but we never got caught staying up studying or acting a fool. There was one time when the floor leader did the check and surprisingly, our residence manager Mr. Hedge did the second check. Mr. Hedge walked in the room, which was pitch black, and began to antagonize me in a way. Now, before I proceed . . . yes . . . my roommates and I were up playing Mario Kart on a laptop and we were having a great time, but he didn't know that! By the time he walked in, we were all on our beds just laying down. For some reason Mr. Hedge walked directly to me, and began talking to me in a rude tone asking what I was doing, and what's going on in here, etc. Due to the harsh tone, I was in utter disbelief that it was him, so I pulled out my cell phone to shine some light to ensure that this was indeed Mr. Hedge, the ministerial major residence manager. He then yelled, "Get that out of my face" and he started being confrontational with me. I remember just laying back down remaining silent and dormant knowing that I didn't have power to do anything about the treatment I was receiving, but he was able to do whatever he wanted to me including kick me out for no reason which would be the worst thing he could do. There was one time where my roommate, the floor leader, had caught me listening to gospel music with drums and he gave me demerits. Being in the forgiving mood, when I saw him after church I said, "I understand what I did and I want you to know that I don't not like you." In times of excitement or anxiety I often misspeak, because I meant to convey that I didn't have a problem with him and that we're still cool even though he wrote me up.

Somehow this message got misconstrued as it was relayed to Mr. Hedge, so one day I was called down to Mr. Hedge's office after lights out. I mean, I was already lying down about to sleep and then a separate floor leader called me out of the room. Once I made it to Mr. Hedge's office, I seen his desk and a chair behind the desk, but other than that I just remember seeing so many suitcases from students who were already kicked out and had to leave things behind. I sat in the chair and then he said to me, "So you told Dan (my roommate) that you didn't like him?" I slightly chuckled, knowing that that was far from the truth, and I started to respond, but I was cut off before I could get a word out. "Oh, so you think this is a joke? You think this is funny? Louie, do you want to be at this school?" Mr. Hedge asked me. By that time, I was shaking in my flip flops! I was on the cusp of losing all that I had gained and all that my mother had worked for, so once again. I had to lie dormant and cowardly make an attempt to convince him of how the situation really unfolded. After the meeting, he took time to confirm with my roommate and verify that the incident was a mere miscommunication. The next semester he took the opportunity to apologize one day when he seen me in passing, but that was the dreadful life that one had to live at PCC. People could come for you at any time, and if you gave in only a little bit . . . the results would be costly.

Mr. Ross was my security boss who was soft spoken, but very strict. I was completely embarrassed one day when he got on my case; the interaction felt similar to the Mr. Hedge incident. I remember him turning red in the face, talking down to me, and embarrassing me in front of my coworkers. I went to class thinking, "man... why did he have to disrespect me like that and talk to me like that? He doesn't do this with anyone else, so why am I getting treated this way. Why do I have to keep dealing with this stuff at this school?" I was so furious, but I tried not to show it. I remember being in class, sitting at my desk with my textbook open, staring at my professor, and trying my best to control my deep breathing and tears that were dropping down my face. Clearly, that was to no avail, because Dr. Devaney, my professor, had to actually stop class and speak with me in the hallway just to talk to me and see what was bothering me. Dr. D was one of my favorite professors along with Mr. Heckel, but that time Dr. D really showed concern for my wellbeing, and he even made a commitment to follow up with my boss to let him know about the impact that he can have on others.

******

My stepfather, Uncle Chibli, passed away when I was at school, but when I came home to comfort my mother before the funeral—we started hearing stories about his side of the family making accusations about my mom. Now Uncle

Chibli and my mother were on the verge of divorce and they were living apart, but he began to have heart failure and, as a loving wife, my mom went to visit him at the hospital several times. He passed away a short while after his hospitalization, but out of the blue, Uncle Chibli's family began making several false accusations saying that my mom poisoned my step father, that she used witchcraft against him, that she pulled the tube from his nose, and there were many other stories they made up. I don't know why this is, but I hear that, according to Liberians, no one dies of natural causes. I can be in America and dying from cancer and someone on the other side of the world will swear that my lover is using witchcraft against me to kill me and take my riches. My Uncle Big Boy was also there to comfort my mother at the time as well. When he heard the rumors he said, "If anyone of them starts saying that foolishness around me—I will slap them." Of course with that being my mother and favorite uncle, I was there by their side ready to back them up. My mind was blown to hear this in general, but as time progressed . . . it came to my attention that my own step brothers were rehearsing these thoughts as well. By the time the wake and funeral came around, the church building was in the midst of an all-out brawl and what I knew as family had suddenly became quickly dismantled.

Even though I was a completely changed man at school... that didn't necessarily translate when I was at home. Don't get me wrong . . . I did my best. I still dressed in the same business casual clothes because my thoughts were—I needed to appear to be someone who is all about peace and "not about that life" (my old life). I listened to gospel music when I picked up my friends and I even witnessed to them *all the time* to where they got tired of hearing me! Eventually however, I would fall back into some of the old activities like drinking and hooking back up with my ex-girlfriend. While that may seem small . . . I had already been conditioned in a way that even those seemingly minor missteps were able to make me feel worlds away from my relationship with God. I wanted all my friends to get saved and experience the fullness of life that I had, but they usually ended up converting me. Cursing, vain conversations, drinking, sex, and hanging out. Since all the gang leadership pretty much got passed on as people went on with their life (I was the only one to go to college as, for the most part, everyone else moved away or was in prison), so my brother Tyrone now had the most rank among the school age folks. He had turned into something vicious too. He started having kids, dropped out of school, and always kept guns on him. All the kids were afraid of him and sucked up to him. Tyrone was drinking early and often, and he was even living on the other side of town with the OGs, or at least, this is what he'd do when I wasn't around or when he got kicked out of our house.

I remember one time when he got kicked out and I had come back for the summer from PCC. Now first off, after I got saved and changed my life, all I could think about was blood-in/blood-out. Violation. I was very terrified about what would happen to me when I ran across the OGs and if they learned that I wasn't down anymore. I actually had visions and nightmares of being in an old rusty apartment bathroom, getting beat up by Prince and others while they stuck my face in a nasty toilet and slammed the seat against my head. Yeah, it was that serious. But when it came to my brother . . . I had to go ahead and face the consequences. Like I was saying before, one day when I was home during summer break and looking for Tyrone, I decided to go to known places where we used to be and lo and behold, there is Prince—walking back from the store. After I parked my car and walked over to him . . . I remember the distinct look on his face as I asked about Tyrone's whereabouts. Prince, a tall, dark, scary figure, stared down at me so hard with this, "Boy if you don't get outta my face with yo sellout ass", face on, but to my amazement, he pointed me in the right direction and I was able to rescue my baby brother.

Interesting enough, the next time I seen Prince I had the chance to witness to him.

I successfully completed PCC though!!! A semester early too (clearly I had to hurry and get out of that place). Since I finished a semester early I began working for juvenile there in Pensacola, taking online classes for my Master's degree at the University of West Florida, and hanging out with my friends who were still at the PCC. I had my own place and even though my friends, who were still in school, weren't supposed to leave campus to go to people's houses . . . I would provide that relief for them either way. One time my good friend Vaughn came over with his roommate and asked if he could store a new television at my house because there was no room for it in his storage at school. Next thing I knew, the police came to my house regarding a stolen television and the school subsequently found out that Vaughn had been to my place, so he got kicked out. I felt bad for my friend, but to top it off—the school proceeded to send me a letter telling me I couldn't walk across the stage for the commencement ceremony! I must admit, I thought that was the end all be all, but I was able to convince them to allow me to participate in the graduation because my family was already coming from Africa and it would mean the world to my mother who sacrificed everything to help her son have a better life than she did. All thanks to God—I won them over and I was able to walk across the stage.

CHAPTER SEVEN

Helping Others

I knew what my career goals were. I worked Campus Security and I interned and volunteered with the Florida Department of Juvenile Justice (FDJJ) while still in school. I would've started my career as a Juvenile Probation Officer off the bat but, since my school was unaccredited at the time, I had to work in the detention center for starters. The State of Florida was paying for six credits a semester for my Master's degree, so I had it made. My plan was to work in juvenile detention until I received my Masters in Criminal Justice Administration and then move over to the probation department. I knew that I only needed five years of work experience and the Masters to attain the position I wanted back home, so I began putting my plan into fruition. I was completely driven and motivated, plus, I was in school full time and I worked over 40 hours each week.

At the juvenile detention center, many of my coworkers became good friends of mine. Two of my favorites were Officer Rivers & Officer Terry. Terry was retired from the Navy and a major Alabama Crimson Tide fan, and Rivers was a good spirited brother from Pensacola. I was the youngest employee at my job and everyone else was about ten years older than me. The craziest, and unluckiest, thing happened to me early in my career. One weekend, while I helped Officer Terry cut trees in his backyard, a tree branch fell on me. I ended up trapped on the top of his roof with a large tree branch practically embedded into my leg and, when I was rushed to the hospital, I found out that I had broken a few bones in my ankle. After that happened, I reported back to my job only to be informed that they would have to terminate my employment, but they did inform me that I could reapply once a position came open once again. Now, of course that wasn't working out for me because I wasn't from the area. I had just graduated from college and got my apartment, the job was paying for my school, and I already laid out my five year plan. There were no guarantees that I would get better or that I would even have enough funds to sustain myself until a new position became available.

I knew something had to be done, so I went to chat with my friends in the probation department. I was hoping they would have some type of payment plan or a connection available for me since I volunteered with them a year prior. The supervisor, Therese Moses, actually helped me in a great way. She coordinated with the employees under her supervision and they all donated some of their sick time to me. They took from their own collection of sick time (which is an equivalent of money for them), and they donated it to me so that I didn't have to lose my job. All I needed to do was get better and return to work. This was such a major blessing in my life. They believed in me enough to sacrifice their own sick days! I was ecstatic! I remember sitting in my boss' office as I was about to read the letter that I wrote to him, begging to keep my job, but he interrupted me with good news. He explained what Therese was able to do for me, and how I was able to stay employed. I dropped the paper on the floor and began crying tears of joy.

I went to the Juvenile Supervision Officer Training Academy in Tallahassee, Florida as soon as my ankle was healed and back to normal. At the academy I became a leader in the class and seen firsthand what it's like to lead people. I found that, for me at least, speaking to and caring for people came naturally and that's mainly what leadership entailed. However, I knew that I also had to maintain a good reputation and character among my classmates as well. When I returned to Pensacola from the academy, I hit the ground running. I had gotten my second chance to earn my way into my desired career field and I wasn't taking it lightly. I actually received an *Officer Of The Quarter* award for the work that I was doing; my supervisors knew that they would expect nothing but the best from me. At that time I weighed around 140 pounds and I'm only 5'7 (not tall), but the kids in Florida are a totally different type of breed from Texas kids. These kids look like grown men! A lot of them had dreadlocks, gold teeth, and weighed a healthy 180 pounds and up... it was an interesting task for me to establish my authority in detention to say the least.

I remember one time with a particular youth—let's call him John. John was not following directions all day. He was horse playing, slapping kids in the back of the neck as jokes, talking in line, etc. After addressing his behavior several times throughout the day, John decided to slap someone while in line and he thought I didn't notice it. So I stopped what I was doing, approached him and told him that this was going to be my last time telling him to stop. John kept a straight face. He looked at me straight in the face and said, "Man… fuck you." I just turned around and carried on about my business.

I started realizing that I was going to have to do a little bit more than my coworkers to successfully get the job done. I was the youngest, the smallest, and most of the kids were my size or bigger. My resolution was to take it back to the LT days. I went to the store and bought a pair of baseball gloves for my back pocket and I began to study the de-escalation policy more closely. I wasn't necessarily looking for the best ways to deescalate situations, but more so how to respond to hostile situations when de-escalation wasn't being effective. Now, physical encounters in the jailhouse were not uncommon. Kids would break the rules all the time and, when it was time to face consequences for it, they normally would refuse to accept them. So if they were told to go to their room to take a break… their response would be, "No, how about you put me in my room!" They were always looking for a fight, so we found ourselves in a dilemma. On one hand—we must maintain safety in the detention, a good learning environment in the school, and we must have a behavior management program that incentivizes good behavior while punishing bad behavior. On the other hand—we didn't want to abuse or purposely hurt the youth. So it's safe to say that early times in the Pensacola Detention were on the rough end. Shortly after a few times of applying the gloves and showing kids that I will operate by the rules and physically assist them into compliance if need be… things eventually began to get better and flow more smoothly. Not only were my physical interactions a game changer, I also began making good use of the reporting system as well. The reporting system provided a snapshot of the youth's behavior in detention to the judge when they showed up for hearings. I found that keeping it fair and providing this knowledge to the kids helped them to make better decisions which ultimately helped my coworkers and I have more successful days.

During those times in Florida I found out that I had a gift of identifying voids and filling them. I was able to make the admissions process more efficient.. What would normally take my coworkers 2-4 hours to complete ended up getting done by me in 30-45 minutes, and I created procedures on the flow of how to get it things done too. I was shining bright like a diamond in Florida, but things suddenly changed on the day I was attacked.

One day we were short staffed, and one of the rules were that two officers must be present on the floor for kids to be out of their rooms. On this day, however, one of the female residents was rushed to the hospital which made our predicament worse. It was still rather early in the morning and we had to make all the kids spend the rest of their day locked in their rooms until the officers, who escorted the young lady, returned to the facility. Even though this was the case, lunch time and dinner time still come around and according to state and federal regulations as well as the law of humanity, *we had to feed the kids.* Interesting enough, being short staffed was nothing new to us. One officer would open the doors and administer the food, and then make the final round to retrieve all the utensils on days like those.

On this particular day, however, I was attacked by a kid who barged his way out of his room after I opened his room door to retrieve his eating utensils. Being that we were short staffed—I was the only officer on the floor at that time, and when I reached for my radio to call a "Code Blue", the radio fell to the floor. This kid proceeded to pick me up and he attempted to slam me on the ground. It was at that point that I knew that I had to regain control of the situation. Now, since I was at work… I couldn't simply beat him up; I knew that I had abide by the rules, especially since everything that we did was on camera. I was able to wrestle the kid off of me, place him down on a table top, and hold his hands down on his chest to keep him calm. Of course he kept attempting to fight me off of him, so when I couldn't control his hands any longer I was forced to place my left hand on his face to hold it down, and I placed my right hand on his right shoulder. I held him down in that position for a few seconds as I repeatedly told him to calm down. After I saw that he was done fighting, I took my hands off of him. My colleagues came to my assistance after the incident had concluded, but as soon as they walked in, one kid, who I had placed in confinement earlier that day for his behavior, began yelling out, "Hey, McClain was choking him!"

I didn't mind what he was saying, because I had a room full of witnesses and the camera was there to back me up as well, so I blew it off. The youth who attacked me even began stating that I choked him after that too, but I had no worries. As I began writing my report, my supervisor called me to the office and what he showed me on the tape totally blew my mind. The department's recording system did not capture events in real time. It would record for about five seconds and then pause for eight seconds and then continue. My mind was blown. To top it off, the camera actually was able to verify everything that I said happened. Unfortunately for me however, from the time when I placed the kid on the table and put his hands on his chest to the time when I placed my hands on his face and shoulder—the camera paused. It actually showed a picture of my transition from his chest to his face, so imagine a snapshot of a kid laying on his back, an officer over him, both of my hands outstretched towards his upper body area. No lie—the camera painted a picture that even made me second guess myself.

They said they were going to terminate me even though they couldn't substantiate the claim of choking. The department conducted an internal investigation, contacted the Department of Families and Children, called the police, and conducted an external investigation. Through all of this, they could not substantiate the claim of choking, so they wrote me up for nine policy violations, which I appealed, but they disregarded my appeal. I was fired from my first job and I was no longer employed with the State Government!

This caused me to slump into a deep depression. For the second time now, I felt things were happening to me that were outside of my control, and I couldn't do anything to hinder them from coming or wrecking my life. Not only did I lose my job, but I lost my school opportunity as well. I had 30/33 credits for my Master's Program and I only needed one more class to be completed. I lost my apartment; I had a girlfriend at the time so I had to leave her behind, and worst of all—I had to move back to my mom's house in Texas. I went to school to learn to how to become a man, to emerge victorious, successful, and to be able to sustain myself. Now, in a twisted turn of events, I lost everything that I worked for and worked towards. Imagine this—my major was in Criminal Justice, I had my whole career planned out before me, but now I was fired from the State Government with an accusation of child abuse held against me. I was so discouraged that I began working for minimum wage at the pretzel shop in the mall when I moved back home. Eventually, my old security boss saw me and said, "Come on man, you could have just asked me and I would have hired you." So I asked and he surely did come through, being a man of his word.

While working for security (mall cop) back in Arlington, my mind was still focused on Juvenile Justice and how I could find my way back into my passion. Ironically, however, I mainly felt defeated. Again, I was fired from the state government, it was my first job, the child protective service opened a case on me (even though it was found to be unsubstantiated), and I just felt that all of this played against me and surely every employer would see this and discard me as a candidate for employment. I was consistently complaining about my situation. But then I had a conversation with a coworker named Galeo Johnson. This was a soft spoken African American gentleman who was a few years older than me and we seldom worked the same shift. One day he challenged me when I was relaying my situation to him.

He said, "Ok Louie. I hear what you're saying about your exploits in the past. I hear you saying the great things you've done and I hear you talking about how you feel defeated, but what are you doing to change those things right now? You can sit in interviews and harp all day about what you've done in the past, but how are you making a difference today? What are you doing now? If there's a will, there's a way. Most of the things you've been saying doesn't mean a thing to today's employer... they want to see what you're actively doing right now. Have you even attempted to work back in that field?"

"Yes I have been trying," I said. "I wasn't selected to move forward with the adult jail job I applied for, I've been filing out applications online, in person, I've visited the detention center and tried to speak with someone, and when

I get someone on phone or in person they always instruct me to go back and apply online... I have been trying man."

"What else could you do", Galeo asked. "Have you considered volunteering?"

And at that point, it was like a light bulb went off in my head. Even though I initially felt challenged, I ended up having a determined spirit. Next thing I knew, I was volunteering with the community service and restitution program in Tarrant County Juvenile (Fort Worth), and I was mentoring at a Dallas County Alternative School.

A few months prior, I reached out to my cousin Aydn who also had a cousin named Frank who just happened to work in Tarrant County (the ultimate destination from my five year plan). Aydn connected Frank and I via telephone and we were able to have a great conversation. He pretty much told me about the job, his role there, and the best ways to look for opportunities. I found this conversation interesting because this was the first time that another person took free time out to have a conversation of this nature. Now Frank didn't help me get hired, but after I had a successful de-escalation interaction while volunteering, I had sealed the deal to use my volunteer supervisor as a reference. Eventually, I got hired with Dallas and Tarrant County, but I decided to focus on full time employment with Tarrant. Dallas and Tarrant County are like night and day—namely because Tarrant has a very good behavior management program and their staff members actually utilize it.

Dallas County was an entirely different story. Granted, in Tarrant I worked in the detention center and in Dallas I worked in a residential program (a place where children get adjudicated [sentenced] for a specified time of 6 – 18 months or more). The success of these types of residential programs rely heavily on a good behavior management system and proper implementation of it by staff, but that just wasn't the case. The kids in Dallas could essentially get away with negative behavior and the staff had their hands tied behind their backs. Writing them up wouldn't deter anything. There were only four solitary rooms for this secure 75 person facility, and the supervisors always second guessed and undermined their staff so the kids felt no restraint in doing whatever they wanted to do. Most of the staff there even voiced that they were there to get a paycheck and go home, but that wasn't the overall vibe in Tarrant County.

By this point, it's clear that I prefer Tarrant over Dallas, but here's the actual reason why. If a kid was adjudicated in Tarrant County, then their system would look over a long list of contracted agencies within and outside state lines that they could send kids to. These were five star facilities who demonstrated the best practices in their metrics. If a kid was adjudicated in Dallas County, their system would send the kids to any of the other seven different county operated residential facilities who had a flawed staff and system similar to my experience when I was employed there. I felt as if we were just housing kids, giving them a slap on the wrist, and turning the blind eye. We were releasing kids back into the community without doing any true rehabilitative measures and leaving the kids to their own devices all the while knowing that they'll be back a second or third time around, or even possibly winding up in prison. That Dallas system is greatly failing the kids, and it's just a pure example of the prison-industrial complex.

Lastly, in Dallas, the adult jail inmates made the lunch (ham sandwiches along with carrots and celery), and shipped them to all the county facilities and that's what we ate. In Tarrant, they had their own cafeteria staff that made fresh, warm, and healthy food for every meal. Tarrant was my clear choice.

After I got settled in at Tarrant County, I took it upon myself to create a nonprofit organization, *Humane Resources*, to help people who have criminal backgrounds get connected to jobs. Here's the gist of what that was about:

Humane Resources' mission was to aid former clients of correctional facilities in finding employment through web-based technology and relationship marketing. Humane Resources would accomplish its mission by:

1. Providing access to an informative website that is full of community organizations in the Dallas / Fort Worth Metroplex whose sole purpose is to provide assistance to former clients of correctional facilities.

2. Presenting and marketing the organization at churches, community organizations, and community events.

3. Meeting with clients for employment consulting purposes.

4. Establishing working relationships with business owners and community stakeholders to further the cause of assisting former clients of correctional facilities.

Our niche was to be an organization that was non-competitive and aimed to collaborate with all reentry programs and community organizations that assist former clients of correctional facilities. Since this matter was close to heart, I wasn't focused on making a profit or taking other reentry programs out of business. The thought was this: people get released from jail or prison every day. When they do, they go to several places looking for jobs and they get turned down. Also, a stipulation of their parole or probation is that they have a job so, if they could be gainfully employed, then that will lessen their chances of getting back involved with criminal behavior. Therefore, I realized that all I needed to do was learn about which jobs and agencies helped or hired people with criminal backgrounds and then point those people in the right direction. It was that simple for me. I traveled throughout the vast parts of Dallas – Fort Worth Metroplex handing out flyers, meeting with stakeholders and community leaders, and I even attended a reentry fair at a Federal prison in Fort Worth. This was the least I could do to give back and, besides, all the people I grew up with had criminal records.

******

In 2010, one of my uncles died in Liberia, so my family traveled there for the funeral. This was my first time ever being in Africa, and all that I had heard prior to being there was the great stories of my parent's childhood. I heard that the place had paved roads, McDonalds, palm trees, beautiful beaches, and how it was practically no different from my experience in America. When I touched down on that soil, however, it was a complete culture shock! I saw people without hands, arms, and legs. I saw struggle, poverty, and suffering in a third world country and, at that point, I was determined at that time to learn more about Liberia; the land of my parents. We were only there for two weeks, but during that time I walked around and observed the culture. I mainly wanted to find a bookstore so I could read more about the history and culture but surprisingly enough… I couldn't find any. I even had a tour guide walking around with me and he couldn't find anything either. Later on, we walked to the University of Liberia…

and couldn't find anything other than textbooks that were being sold. I was surprised!

Ironically, after a few days of finding nothing, I suddenly came across a book that covered Liberia's history while I was getting something from my aunt's closet. I read the chapter about Liberia from Martin Meredith's book, *The Fate of Africa*. Over the next few days when I'd gotten the chance to complete the chapter—my heart had dropped down to the soles of my feet and I literally cried real, heavy tears after learning of all that the country had been through. I was about to turn 25 years old in a few days, and even up to that point I had no idea that the place where my parents were from had endured so much.

I learned about the forceful takeover by freed slaves, the 150 years of a one party rule which marginalized the indigenous people, a coup which overtook the government and killed the President (who was my great uncle), the ten years of chaos that followed and left thousands killed, raped, homes looted, and people fleeing the entire nation. After the ten years of chaos, there was the infamous fourteen years of outright civil war with child soldiers raiding towns with machine guns, being high off drugs, raping, killing, and plundering. I was informed that rebel soldiers were the ones responsible for the people who I'd noticed with missing body parts. The soldiers barbarically chopped them off. I witnessed the children who had to live through this chaos… needless to say; I couldn't stop the tears from flowing for my people. I immediately felt an obligation to do something to stop the pain and turn the tide. I recall being around a nearby water well where a bunch of school aged kids were to get water to take to their families. I remember meeting a young girl who couldn't be any more than six years old at the time;

I assumed she was retrieving water for her family at the water well. After she performed her task, I politely asked her if she wanted take a picture and, to my surprise, she nodded and said yes. As I proceeded to take the picture, the girl just blankly stared into the camera. I waited a while for her to smile, but nothing happened. I then said, in my Liberian accent, "But you can't smile?" She then gave a little smirk for the camera and then walked away from me after I took the picture. I couldn't get that phrase out of my head from that day forward: smile, Liberia. Smile.

As a project of Humane Resources, my US based 501c3 nonprofit organization, I created Liberia Smile to do a few things; here it is:

The mission and vision of the *Project: Liberia Smile* stands in unison with the hearts and minds of all Liberians who desire a more beautiful and prosperous country. Our mission is to provide an opportunity to high school seniors, who lack the opportunity to receive a college education because of the lack of financial assistance from their families, and train them to mediate conflicts that include land tenure issues, gender issues, and other forms of religious and tribal biases. Furthermore, Liberia Smile's vision is for Liberia to be restored to its former beauty and to be rid of the stigma of being a war-torn country. Scholarship recipients will be encouraged to play active roles in the reconstruction of Liberia as it relates to the improvement of the social, moral, political, and economic development. This will be done by providing thought provoking and inspirational leadership skills geared towards the elimination of bigotry, tribalism, nepotism, corruption, and all other forms of abuse of power in the effort to make Liberia an example of peace and gender equality in Africa and the world.

******

Remember . . . . I had a five year plan setup for Tarrant County but, due to the circumstances, my five year plan came into fruition in less than two. Even though there was a lot of struggle leading up to it, I was able to look back and see how it all worked out for the better. I began learning about all the policies and procedures at Tarrant County Juvenile. I was thrilled to be back in a line of work that's aligned with my passion, but I also wanted to ensure that I never found myself in a similar situation like the one I experienced in Florida. From that time I became the guy who started constructing policies and procedures and repairing old ones that were outdated or had any grey areas. I joined leadership committees, I trained people on policies and procedures, gave departmental motivational trainings, and I facilitated groups with the youth. I learned a lot in those times from two outstanding colleagues, Adam Hill and Said Muhammad. These two were pillars in the Tarrant County detention at that time who taught me early on that I needed to operate differently than how I operated in Florida.

I was so accustomed to the threat of physical violence in Florida that I almost even welcomed it at times, but the staff at Tarrant were complete geniuses at de-escalation. After witnessing heart pouring and abasing moments where Said and Adam would reach kids who were struggling with certain behaviors, it blew my mind how they were able to turn the whole situation around. They also gave the best 15 – 30 minute group meetings of life changing content straight from the top of their heads. Most people only saw negative behavior in the children we served, but these gentlemen taught me to see way more. They taught me how to pay attention to the kid's audience in detention, and to understand their living situations as well. I learned that, in most cases, these kids had to fend for themselves. Many of them lost loved ones due to drugs, gangs, or prison and, at the end of the day, these were kids at heart who were doing the best they could to cope within their circumstances. These are things that I've always felt and read about, but for the first time... I was placed around strong men who held these truths in high esteem. Adam and Said lived their lives, each day, breaking into the hearts and minds of these kids to impact change in their lives. Tarrant County is the most honorable place I've ever worked at. I see many people succeed in their businesses, whether if it's entrepreneurship, selling cars, or being corporate executives, but I never wanted to know what life was like for them. I only wanted to follow the lead of the good brothers at Tarrant, and make a difference in the lives of troubled youth. While working there I learned how to reach the kids and how to talk them out of making bad decisions, including suicide. I learned how to really give all of myself, get one on one, and listen to the cries and concerns of the kids. If they sat on the couch, then I'd do the same. If they sat on the floor, then I'd sit next to them. If they went straight to their room and slammed the door, I'd open the door sit on their bed and give them the opportunity to let it all out. I loved every single aspect about my job. I was living life the way I wanted to and I was in a position to make a difference every single day.

Even though I was living paycheck to paycheck, I can honestly say I was living stress free. During those days, I worked five days a week at the juvenile hall and would be off on Tuesdays and Wednesdays. On my off days I would take 4 to 8 hours on one of my off days to work on Humane Resources or Liberia Smile and, since I was at my dream job,

I really didn't fret about the financial strain outside of the fact that I was constantly seeking promotions within the juvenile facility and not getting them. I bounced from apartment to apartment doing my best to maintain a place to stay and there was actually a time when I lived with a coworker for over a year. My mother's house was still available and she would always encourage me to live with her, but my manly pride wouldn't let me. Well, pride was only one dynamic. My mother's boyfriend had also played a factor too. She started seeing this guy a couple years after my step father passed and I wasn't feeling him at all. I would wake up to him talking on the phone early in the morning and hear pots banging around in the kitchen while he tried to hustle a meal for himself. Meanwhile the kitchen floor would be filled with dirt and grime, the dishes wouldn't be washed, and the entire place would be a mess. I would wake up at times like this and immediately become really angry with my heart pounding inside of me. I kept my mouth shut for my mother's sake (who was always working 2-3 jobs still), but I was patiently waiting for him to speak badly towards my mother… no need to go into further detail. The two of them, nevertheless, had positive interactions, but that was the reason why I stayed out of that house. It was for my own sanity.

Ever since I moved back to Texas I was looking for many ways to get involved with the community and, since I had recently lost my job and seemingly my entire career field, I was looking for learning and business opportunities to dive into. I learned about this community-based organization called the Urban League which had a local chapter for Young Professionals that I would fit in perfectly with, so I joined. Also, my cousin Aydn, who was working on his doctorate back then, would host informal meetups with a few other cousins and friends. We would put all of our goals on a white board to further map them out and create concrete plans to work towards making it become a reality. The main participants were Aydn, Ivor, Koosh, and I. At that time, Ivor had a music company that taught kids how to play the piano at certain schools. Koosh was still trying to find his way while still working in the banking industry, Aydn was working on school and dreaming of owning a consulting firm, and I had Humane Resources, Liberia Smile, and juvenile in my arsenal. Those meetings were very impactful because they kept us focused. Ivor is a millionaire now; he has multiple pharmacies and he also does business in Hollywood. Aydn consults for Ivor and other companies and is well established with his practice in uptown Dallas, Koosh works for a major IT company and also operates a music production studio in Liberia, and as for me, I own the largest culturally competent publishing firm in the world: Melanin Origins. I guess what I'm saying here is that it is very refreshing to look back on those humble times and see where we all are today. Paycheck to paycheck is never ideal, but none of us back then allowed our current circumstance to determine where we were headed in the future.

Now, even though I had some very positive and influential family members and business associates, I still made time for the guys that I grew up with. Not as often, but we made time for each other especially when I was burnt out from all of the constant toil and effort that I was putting in and hardly seeing any results. Honestly, I actually felt that I wasn't seeing the results fast enough. I decided that I was working myself too hard and, since I wasn't getting promoted and things weren't progressing the way I wanted,

I started to spend more time with my family and friends, who I moderately neglected as I was pursuing my goals. So I would catch up with Mike, Garwin, Koosh, and Ced every now and then to have a drink or go out to a club to meet people. In that unforgettable time, I picked up roller skating and began to play the guitar more too. I love playing the guitar and many people adore that, but most don't know how the skating scene is out here in Dallas. Depending on where you're from in the U.S., you may view skating in a wide array of ways. First let me say that I'm not referring to roller blading... I mean the quad, non-inline roller skates and I'm talking about simulating choreography to hip-hop and R&B on the rink floor! Many people who were ages 21-45 were coming together to have this type of fun on weekdays and weekend nights. It was refreshing to encounter so many avenues to live a positive life.

Everything was going along very smoothly until the one day came that changed everything. It was a Tuesday and I was off, so I woke up and did some cleaning up at the place I was living at. After lunch, I ventured to my mother's house to see her after she got off of work. I sat in the couch there, opened my new book, "The Art of War" and proceeded to read. The first chapter of The Art Of War begins by discussing "conflict". It states that in order for there to be an emergence of a great leader . . . there must be conflict. It paints conflict as, not only a necessary element of life, but a good element that is potentially the only means available to witness the necessary change that one is wishing to see. It talks about how revolutions began through conflict, about how countries were formed, and how love is solidified. It shared a perspective with me that I will never forget.

My mother eventually came home and, as I did when I was a kid, I rushed down the stairs to greet her. We chatted for a few moments, and while I don't remember the exact conversation, I do remember the glaring look of satisfaction that she had with her son. She was just looking at me with a smile that said, "I am so proud of the man my son has become." The rest of that day went by so fast, but I still remember it like it was yesterday. I went to my boy Garwin's house directly after I left my mom's place. We played dominoes, had a few drinks, and then we went to a local lounge to meet up with friends. After having a good time there, I dropped Garwin off back home and proceeded to my place only to get pulled over by the police for speeding in a construction zone, and subsequently, I was arrested and hauled off to jail for driving while intoxicated. The next morning I woke up in a jail cell with one word reverberating through my mind: *conflict.*

CHAPTER EIGHT

The Reconstruction Period

Before I move forward I want it to be clear that I was wrong to drink and drive; I'm responsible for everything that followed that incident. The police officer who pulled me over had a long history of over 300 DWI arrests in that small city, and he had a reason for pulling me out of my vehicle to test me. As I was reaching in the glove box for my insurance, he leaned into my vehicle to simulate himself sniffing into my car as my back was turned. According to the officer, that half a second whiff of the interior of my car reeked of alcohol even though there weren't any open containers in the vehicle. This is what my attorney relayed to me during the court process, but I understand—some people's pores reek of alcohol when they drink. Even though I question the motives and tactics of the officer, I take 100% of the blame for putting myself and others in danger by driving while intoxicated.

After I got my DWI, life resumed and I went back to work. I already knew that, since I had a job in the criminal justice field, my manager could easily find out about the arrest so, when I got back to work, I scheduled a meeting with the Director Ron Lewis and he empathized with my situation. Mr. Lewis is an African-American man who also beat the odds, and he definitely understood my pain. I mean—we all did similar things. We worked hard and once in a while we had after work shindigs with coworkers or friends where alcohol was involved. The conversation I had with the director was a good and comforting one, but reality was still staring me right in the face. Ron informed me on which steps he was going to take and he explained that the department couldn't let me go without a guilty verdict. When I heard that, I wanted to postpone all my court dates and push this *inevitable* verdict as far back as possible, but I knew I didn't have the funds to do that.

I heard there was an attorney who represented a Tarrant County judge who was arrested for a DWI and won the case some time back, so I made it my business to find out who that lawyer was. Once I did, I made an appointment and he agreed to accept my case *and* he even provided me a 50% discount since I was a County employee. Overall, the whole court process was about nine months long. My attorney ensured that I got a good start on the community service and treatment programs as soon as possible so we could present the best case to the judge. I had to take a substance abuse assessment where I was judged to be low risk. I had to attend Alcoholics Anonymous where I saw firsthand what it was like to truly be an alcoholic. Now, most people who are addicted to anything are in denial, but if I learned one thing about alcoholics it's this: there is not one clear definition. An alcoholic can be a person who goes months without drinking and leads a highly successful life, but if a drop of alcohol reaches his/her tongue then they will continue to drink until they pass out. Once they begin drinking, they cannot bring themselves to stop. Another alcoholic is the type that is chemically dependent on it to the point where they have to maintain a certain level of it throughout the day. Alcohol is a must first thing in the morning, on lunch breaks, after work, before bed, and possibly several other times in between. Another type of alcoholic is the type who believes that they cannot have fun without alcohol, so if I'm hanging out with friends at night . . . I'm the bored one because I'm not drinking. And then there are more types—even the kind that will avoid paying important bills, rent, and mortgages just to maintain their drinking habits.

What I learned was that I might have possibly been in the category of the one who desired alcohol in order to have fun, so while people were sharing their stories . . . I never judged them. I only focused on correcting my own behavior. For all of this I was given one year probation but, before that began, I still had to go to work and perform. I still had to hold my head high in order to comfort, console, and encourage the kids I was working with while knowing that my life was breaking down in front of me. I was depressed and I couldn't even tell the coworkers I was close with, so I had to fake the funk. When the time drew near for me to quit my job, due to my upcoming conviction, I lied to my bosses and coworkers and told them that I got hired at a prestigious bank, and that I was onto a different career path. "But Louie", they said, "you always said how much you wanted to make a difference and how this was your dream job, what about all that?" My response was always the same, "Hey you know . . . I think I'll have more opportunities for growth in the banking industry and when my finances are better . . . I'll be able to volunteer or find my way back." My whole life was a lie at that point, and no one even knew, except for Frank and my mother. It was a harsh reality that I had created for myself and the self-hatred that accompanied it ate away at my soul daily.

It was like a knife in my heart and I felt it every single day. I was like "This is my passion: to work with kids and help transform their lives, to see them where they are, struggling, and to be that light for their dark world." Even though they eventually had to go back to that dark world, I could at least plant a seed. It literally was lifesaving and life changing to work with kids in the juvenile system. After I told Ron the news about the DWI, I walked over to Frank's office to tell him about it as well. He was let down about the situation, but not as if *I* disappointed him. He genuinely felt bad for me. Frank was the main one I trusted and he was there for me just like how I was there for the kids at work. I would seldom go to his house, and we would just sit back and talk about many interesting topics. His words of wisdom always drew me closer to him, because he was never judgmental. Frank was always optimistic, and he was always there to console me. I told him, "ever since I knew what I wanted to do with my life—I created a pathway. I set my goals and worked towards achieving them and I was successful for the most part." I broke my foot and bounced back, I got fired from my first professional job and bounced back, but now with this criminal conviction—I felt like it was literally the end. Everything I worked for was going down the drain, and I didn't know what to do or how to do anything about it. I was lost and didn't know how to gain control of my life. I felt so defeated but Frank's response was simple: move forward. He said, "In life sometimes we don't know exactly where we're going or what we're going to be doing, but we have to continue to *move forward*". At first, I didn't know how to take that. I was still stuck with the fact that the DWI will displace me from the life I envisioned for at least five to ten years and I was in the depths of depression. Yes, I had my degree, but it was from an unaccredited college! Aside from encouraging the youth, I didn't even know what I was good at. I didn't have a father to teach me trades or how to be skillful with my hands. Everything I've done in life, I stumbled upon and was barely able to make due. Now that I've lost everything . . . what was next for me?

Once my court day came in November 2012, I had my mother there by my side. My loving mother has been with me through it all and she has always been my rock; always there to support me. The lawyer pushed my court date back as much as he could to help me try to get another job to sustain myself since we knew my position at Tarrant would end soon, but nothing fell through. I filled out scores of applications only to get rejection after rejection. After I left juvenile I called a good friend of mine named Cynthia Nevels, an outstanding consultant who contracts with the government and large corporations. Cynthia actually helped me with the business plan and federal application for Humane Resources, which at this point was now a past endeavor since current life situations had me broken in shambles. I reached out to her to ask if she knew of any companies that were hiring and I told her about my situation. She then advised me that her consulting firm was hiring part timers and that she would teach me more about the business world, so of course I gladly accepted. It was part time and it was $6 less than what I was making prior, but I had one option only: *move forward*. I began my new job at CynthiaNevels.com as a Business Development Specialist. Working for Cynthia taught me how to network, the basics of business creation, finding your niche, seeking mutually beneficial relationships, and how innovation is key. I learned how to add value to other people's platforms as well. I was very grateful for the opportunity, but I was still putting in applications for better options. Then one day my best friend Jenne called and told me that Geico and American Airlines were hiring. Now, I really wanted the Geico job because they paid a decent wage, but I didn't make the cut for them. American Airlines called me back and offered a position making $10.86—over $5 pay cut from my previous job in juvenile, but again, I knew only one thing at that time: *move forward*. The position was in a call center and the job included sales, which I felt as if I was a horrible salesman, but I took it nonetheless.

Here's what I learned about networking—there's an art to it. While working with Cynthia, I learned all about Cynthia's products and services, the reason why she exists, the organizations she helped boost efficiency and profits for, etc. in an effort to be able to communicate our value to potential clients. However, my first networking experience taught me something even more valuable about the networking process. All of that information can be very useful, but without relationship building through learning about the potential client then you're wasting your time. I went to my first business mixer and approached a group of guys and girls who all had a mixed drink in their hand and were talking and laughing as if they knew each other. As soon as I got in the crowd, they all sort of turned to me, so I introduced myself and gave a quick fire 45 second elevator pitch about CynthiaNevels.com and they all seemed impressed. For about five seconds. Someone in the group said, "Thank you Louie. It's nice meet you" and then they all went back to their non-business talk and laughed together again. After that I just moseyed away from that crowd.

Networking is all about the art of adding value to another while seeking a mutually beneficial relationship. It's best to not go directly for the sale or discuss pertinent business jargon at the first meetup, but let's get back to the story. After I got the DWI, I was still trying to do a lot to keep myself busy in a constructive way. I practically taught myself how to play the guitar better, and I subsequently wrote over thirty songs. Sensing that I had something special in my hands, I decided to seek out other musicians and artists to practice and record with. Eventually I had a band created and a couple singers to sing my songs as well. Again, this is practically how I kept myself busy back then. When I successfully completed my probation, I released my songwriter demo entitled *All Dues Paid*. I named it that for a number of reasons.

1. I felt that I had dedicated my life to service and helping mankind.
2. Even with all the service and dedication, I kept getting negative results, so I thought I'd done enough and my debt to society was paid.
3. I literally had paid all my probation dues and I had successfully terminated my probation.

Now in all honesty, my contribution to the world at that point may seem like a drop in the bucket, but in my world . . . I had dedicated my whole life. I contributed to making many positive changes with troubled youth in the juvenile system. I talked kids out of suicide, and I also comforted a young man after his mother died of AIDS before he was shipped off to prison for over ten years after shooting another kid. I've consoled a lot of kids, and I've been a witness to many of their problems. I remember a young lady who was only 13 years old and hooked on heroin; it was a sad sight to see. I wouldn't wish any child to go through that type of pain and addiction. There was another young lady who was at the wrong place at the wrong time and was now on trial for murder, and many more in that realm. I was more than a supervision officer at work. I was a confidant, a friend, a safe place, a counselor, and a lighthouse that illuminated and uplifted young spirits. With all the work I did for the formerly incarcerated, the disadvantaged kids in Liberia, and with all the mentorship programs I was involved in… I felt that I had performed enough good deeds. I tried to help so many people in so many different ways that I had paid all of my dues to society. On the day of the release of my demo, I gathered all my mentors and took them out to eat—now remember, these guys knew nothing about what I was going through, but it was just a way for me to celebrate my accomplishments which, to them, was a CD release. Only Frank and I knew that it was something way more.

Now that I was hired at American Airlines, a glimmer of hope appeared and I was excited about the new opportunity even though it didn't pay the same as Juvenile did. I was living with my mother again, but I was blessed to have the new full time job that allowed me to have flight benefits to travel the world without spending a dime! Damn right I was excited! But then . . . . BOOM! One day when I was in church, I received a text notification that said, "Did you nut in me?" At that time I already knew. I was freaking mortified and my heart dropped to the soles of my feet once again. After conversing with the person who turned out to be the mother of my daughter, and, after I learned that she was already four months pregnant, I had to come to terms with the fact that I would be expecting a child in the upcoming fall. Interesting enough, when I learned of this information, I was already in a relationship with someone else so I had to break the news to her. Thank God she understood since there was no infidelity involved, but just a few months after that, she became pregnant as well. After all that had taken place, now I had added fuel to the flame that was already consuming my life. I was now expecting two kids, out of wedlock, from two women, who were due six months apart. I thought about ending my life many times. I felt like such a horrible person and the depression sunk in even more. *Why me?* Is the question I kept asking God. What did I do that was so horrible to deserve this? I thought the DWI was my lowest point, but when it became evident that I was the one destroying my life, I didn't know how to deal with that. On at least two occasions, I swallowed a handful of pills . . . . hoping for death. Many nights I cried in my bed while my brain was pointing me to the gun in my storage room. MANY NIGHTS! I mean . . . . I was a criminal once, then I got saved and dedicated my life to helping others, and the results were killing me, so why not just end it myself?

My kids are a blessing and I love them, but at that point in my life I hated myself for introducing them to the world in this way. As for my daughter's mother, once she broke the news to me I immediately went to go visit her and I laid everything out on the table so we both could have a proper understanding of my situation, what to expect, and how we could move forward. I told her that I was there to support her and I was also in a relationship, so we wouldn't be getting together, but I'll always be there for my daughter. When it came to my son's mom I stayed with her because:

1. We were still together
2. My son was coming
3. Even though things hadn't been working out between us, I felt like no girl was going to want to be with me because of my situation
4. I was still broke

I figured that I just had to do what I had to do to somewhat contain the mess that I had created in my life. I tried my best to make things work with her, but I wasn't happy with my life, and I couldn't find a way to be happy in the relationship given the circumstances. We eventually called it quits. The hardest part of it was not being able to wake up to my son every morning and put him to sleep each night, but I believe that it was a sacrifice that I had to make. I couldn't allow him to grow up in a household where two dysfunctional people are always at odds. I knew that both of my children deserved better. My daughter was already with her mother most of the time, but we alternated weekends or weekdays based on my work schedule.

******

At American Airlines I started with a very low rank and pay, but the plan in the company was to move up and progress. Each promotion yields a 10-15% raise and there are many opportunities for promotion. So I scaled the company and created a plan to increase my revenue. One way was through sales at my current position, now remember - I felt that I sucked in sales. I never liked to argue, I didn't have good comebacks, and if you told me no . . . I'd just be like— ok. So, selling is something I always stayed away from, but something clicked when I was in my initial training. We were going to be promoting a credit card. Now, I knew how I thought about credit cards and I knew how most of my friends and their families viewed them too—negatively. I knew that it is a good thing to have one or two to build your credit score, but my friends shied away from it and were very afraid of them. But it clicked to me, the type of people who would be calling into *this* call center are nothing like me or my friends. I literally said this in training, "The people who are calling in are not individuals who are as broke as me." It clicked to me that this is a whole other demographic and that the law of probability will prevail! If I could just get excited about presenting the offer and learn the keywords to say to ethically move the customer into action, then I could experience success. The thing about that way of thinking is that I did experience success and great success at that! I started getting recognitions and monthly bonuses ranging from $300-$600. I started getting offers to join leadership at executive dinners. I even won gift cards and a trip to Sea World!!! Things were looking up, and I even found a new strength within myself because I never believed that I could accomplish these things and find success in these areas. After I was with the company for a year I decided not to renew my commitment to that department, which would have given me a 15% raise and lock me in my current position for another year. I decided to look for other opportunities; I needed to increase my revenue and learn about other aspects of the company.

I took a job in the Crew Scheduling department at American Eagle which was a promotion greater than the average 15%. Funny thing is that I knew nothing about anything in the aviation world back then. I didn't know what crew scheduling was or how to identify different types of airplanes, and I didn't know the difference between

American Eagle and American Airlines. What I did know was how to follow money and that I could learn anything that I applied myself to. I got the job for Eagle by responding to an internal posting while working with American, so even though I got the monetary promotion I was seeking, it was seemingly a demotion to a smaller airline carrier. Also, shortly after I got hired with Eagle they changed their name to Envoy and ceased the working agreement that allowed both companies to share the same American Airlines benefits. However, once I got in the operation center for my new job, I scaled that job field as well. I saw that promotion opportunities were available in crew scheduling, but there's only so far that one could go. That's when I learned about Aircraft Dispatch, a position that is also in the operations center where I was working. Aircraft Dispatchers create the flight plan for each flight which determines the flight routes, takeoff and landing times, approximate fuel for the trip, and more. Dispatchers are 50/50 liable with the pilot for all aspects of the flight while enroute. Many people do not know of this profession, as it is saturated with over 80% older white males, but Aircraft Dispatchers at American Airlines have a starting pay of $80k a year and can make over $150k with overtime. What did you think I would do? I went to Dispatch School! Getting my dispatch certification was a grind because I had my kids to take care of, I had my job to remain dedicated to, and I had to go to class in which learning the subject matter was intense. Lucky for me, my kid's mothers understood my situation, and I was able to take the classes with no external concerns. I'm very thankful to them for that.

I earned my certification in dispatch after only seven months of working at Eagle but, shortly after that, a position came available to be with American Crew Scheduling in Pittsburgh, PA . . . and it was a $14k raise. So I had to make a choice. I could wait for an Eagle dispatch position to become available, and get the experience which would propel me into a more lucrative dispatch career downline with American; or I could go back to the main company to earn more money and be in a better position, today, to take care of my kids. I chose the latter. From the time I became employed with American, the company was already undergoing the merger with U.S. Airways, so going to Pittsburgh was one of the steps along the company's strategic plan. All I knew was that I was finding new growth and success in my life and things just kept looking brighter. In addition to that, moving away from home has always been my salvation. I have always been very excited to get away from the normalcy that I've seen destroy many time and time again. All of the back and forth I was doing to hustle enough money for my kids, all the constant picking up, dropping off, and having no leisure outside of being with my kids, and lastly all of the relationship turmoil I was experiencing with my kid's mothers took a huge toll on me. It was definitely time for a scenery change. Don't forget, I was still broke before I went to Pittsburgh and I still lived at my mom's house too. My kids didn't have adequate insurance and I was tempted to use the system just as I seen others who were getting away with it all their lives so, to say the least, Pittsburgh was an opportunity to breathe and build.

It was very refreshing to have a company send you to a different state, pay for your hotel, pay for your rental car, and pay you per diem for food and miscellaneous expenses. I was finally able to buy clothes that I wanted for business and leisure, eat the food I wanted, and even go to the barbershop again. Speaking of eating what I wanted, up until that time, I ate T.V. dinners for lunch along with a cheap burrito, a back of 25cent chips, and water.

Everything that I was working towards at that point was for the welfare of my two children which I love with all my heart. Every time my son is sleeping I always tell him in his ear, "Daddy loves you. Daddy will always be there for you." I do this every opportunity I have because I need his subconscious to be filled with love and for him to always know that his daddy is here for him. Serenity is like my best friend and she symbolizes redemption to me. In spite of all the things I was going through, when she was born I was filled with so much inexplicable joy. Even when there were times where I was frustrated, or couldn't be the fun and playful dad she was used to seeing, *no matter what,* every time I came back to her she was always smiling when she saw me. If I was ever down or having a bad day, she would come up to me and hug me and pat my back. It's as if she has an innate ability within her to notice the suffering of others and heal them, even as a one year old child. I love both of my kids. They encourage me, they motivate me, and when I was depressed they were one of the main reasons why I did not act on my suicidal thoughts. Before them, my mother was the reason why I wouldn't do it, but now my children were my salvation. I knew I had to live for them and that my absence would be detrimental to their lives. I'm not into perpetuating stereotypes or repeating harmful cycles.

I remember when my son's mom, Toya, was pregnant. She had just begun a new job and they were not offering maternity leave, so when she told me this I did what I had to do. I sought part time employment at several places, and only got accepted at a local restaurant as a dishwasher. Bills had to get paid and I needed to fill in the void with savings to be in the best position to care for my kids. Even still, that was my most embarrassing and humiliating job ever. I have a college degree, I work in corporate America, and now I have an uneducated manager and high school students (employees) bossing me around, throwing dirty dishes at me, and telling me when I can leave for the night. I didn't finish work until 2AM some nights just to be at work the next morning at 8AM. It was a tough time, but I did what was necessary.

During these times Serenity's mom gave me so much trouble. She started arguments for no reason; she cursed me out almost every time she saw me until Serenity was a little over a year old. She always asked me why did I get her pregnant. I was like, "come on man; can't we get over this and move forward?" But that's just the way things were. I remember this one time when I contacted her so I could pick up Serenity, and she said that she didn't have gas to meet up. I then offered to pay for her gas and she agreed. From the moment we pulled up to the gas station, I was all kinds of bitches, motherfuckers, and everything in between. She was yelling all these things while I was literally pumping her gas, taking my daughter out of her arms, and driving off. It was ridiculous, but I put myself in that position so I just had to manage it the best I could. Yet, it always appeared that there was nothing I could do as this unpredictable life was impacting me. I strongly desired custody of my daughter because I wanted to always be with her and provide for her. Also, I didn't want to deal with someone who uses her as a pawn to get what she wants. I didn't want to deal with all the unknowns of the whole "hot one minute cold the next" dynamic with her mother either, because I was being emotionally dragged for no reason with no sign of her letting up. Serenity's mother never took Serenity to get her shots after she was born, and not due to any religious beliefs either. I actually had to bribe her on one occasion with tax money just so she could take Serenity to get her shots. I would have Serenity for an extended amount of time and she would hardly communicate with me for weeks and sometimes months on end, but when she would reach out to spend a day or so with her, she would ask me for child support money the next day as if she's been the sole provider. Through all the times I would have Serenity; however, I'd never ask her for money or assistance to do anything. There were too many unknowns with that whole dynamic when Serenity was away from me including: not knowing if she was being properly clothed, fed, and in the safest environment that could be provided.

I remember having a nervous breakdown at my job and crying profusely in my manager's office due to Serenity's mother blatantly refusing to allow me to see her. I always paid our agreed amount when it came to child support fees and I was always available to spend time with her during the agreed upon times, but there were many times when, for no apparent reason, Serenity's mother would refuse to let me see her. Now, let me be fair here. There was never a time when my actions were uncomely towards her or when I disrespected her to her face, but I did have to set the record straight with her a few times and tell her how I felt about her actions and the way she was treating me during disagreements over the phone. There were times when the words I used towards her were harsh which ultimately contributed to why she would do some of the things she did.

******

When President Barack Obama was elected many of the closet racist came out of the woodworks! Imagine that, hating the man who holds the highest office in the country solely because he's African-American. Then you had Trayvon Martin, Mike Brown, Sandra Bland, and all the other police killings of the generation and, at that time, social media was the main platform where discussions about the issues impacting our nation would be had. I was a part of a Facebook group for the Criminal Justice alumni from PCC and they were posting all kinds of racial epithets calling young Trayvon Martin a thug. There was no evidence that pointed to Trayvon Martin being a thug, but they'd already painted that picture in their minds and plastered it all over social media. He was just a young teen who walked to the store to get candy like every other American teenager. The Criminal Justice alumni from PCC were also posting pictures of *Planet of the Apes* to describe the black people protesting in Ferguson, MO, and continued to spew all kinds of crazy negative things towards people of color. When I would chime in to ask why they were doing this, and say: "Don't you know that this stuff happens to people who look like me *just because* they look like me." "Don't you know this could happen to me?" But they didn't care. They chopped me down with their words, disregarded me, ganged up on me, and some even blocked me as their friend. And most of these are the same people who I used to study with before class; we worked together in groups, and there was even a guy who I used to pray with in prayer group for the first couple years of school who displayed his white supremacists views on social media. I was losing my classmates, my friends, and all faith in befriending white people. At that point I made up my mind that this is how white people are. It doesn't matter how much fun you can have in class, or on the job, or in the gym. When they get home they're going to vote against you and when you get killed in the street—they won't give a damn.

While I still think the previous statement is true to an extent, I do know that as a person of color, you have to rise above that level of thought. We have to. As an individual that's cognizant of your own purpose in life, you can't act the same way with the same level of hate, disgust, and immaturity. We are called to love, we are not called to hate. We are called to change the world and living eye for an eye is not how that gets accomplished. But back then, at least for a short period of time, I decided not to deal with white people at all, but to focus on building with my own. I began listening to Dr. Boyce Watkins and Dr. Umar Johnson and I began learning more about my historical leaders in black American history. For instance, I didn't know that Booker T. Washington and his students built the Tuskegee Institute, which is now called Tuskegee University. This university was built with their bare hands and that's how the whole university exists today. Dr. Umar Johnson taught me that. Furthermore, Dr. Boyce spoke about financial literacy and building your own business to stimulate the black economy. These were awesome, influential men for me during those times.

******

Since my financial situation had greatly improved from the Pittsburgh promotion, I began looking for my house when I went home to visit on weekends, and I was able to secure one just as I transitioned back to Texas from Pittsburgh.

I unofficially had custody of Serenity before I went to Pittsburgh and my mother and aunt helped take care of her while I was away. Nelda, Serenity's mother, and I agreed upon this because she said that she had an opportunity to work in New York. Now this isn't the first time she was supposed to leave the state for work, so I simply told her each time—"ok fine" or "that's cool, congrats!" "You go ahead and get settled and I'll hold on to Serenity so you can focus on getting acclimated to your new location." None of the previous opportunities went through for her, but she did agree to allow me to have unofficial custody the last time, even though she never actually left the state. So all in all, I was the custodial parent during the time I was in Pittsburgh and when I was set to come back home to Texas, I was fretting about how daycare would play out for me with my new demanding schedule. But either way, I moved into my first home and, out of fear, I decided to get back with my son's mother for a smooth transition and, hopefully, a good future with my whole family in one home. That lasted for about a month and a half and we both agreed that we should just go our separate ways once again.

After Toya, my son's mother, and I broke up I began dating a girl who was introduced to me by one of my coworkers and it was something special. You see, going to Pittsburgh meant a lot to me, my whole life was beginning to turn around, all of my mistakes and failures were starting to be overshadowed by exploit after exploit, and I was regaining confidence in myself and hope in the Lord. Lastly, I finally was in a place where Toya and I understood that we wouldn't be together and I felt free! So meeting Shayla was like the icing on the cake. It was like the summit of my life. It was like God was saying, "Louie, you went through all this so that you can achieve this level of love." And it was awesome love too. We laughed, we joked, she helped with Serenity when I needed, and I was a father figure to her son as well. Our kids loved each other and I just knew she was going to be my wife. She had beautiful dark skin, long natural hair, outstanding conversation; she had it all. Even though I was still learning how to manage the dynamic situations with the mothers of my children, being with Shayla was a great help and she took my mind away from all the negativity that was still trying to consume me.

During tax season, Nelda would tell me to claim Serenity on my tax return and then she would tell me to give her $1,200. Now I already knew that $1,200 was the maximum amount you could claim per child, so it didn't bother me to help her out. I can't judge motives, but I'm sure she thought she was "sonning" me by doing that, but I knew that she probably needed it more than I did and I was willing to do anything to avoid issues with the mothers of my children. So when tax season came around in 2016 she told me she'd expect the money. I then told her that that was the agreement we had when *she* had custody of Serenity, but since I had custody of her for over a year by then, it wasn't going to work that way this time around.

Prior to her getting in contact with me for tax money, she hadn't seen her daughter in over three months! And prior to that she would drop by the babysitter to see her for a few minutes or get her for a day and a half and drop her back off for three weeks or more. So when I told her that I won't be able to give her money, she got mad and started to curse me out. Around that time, I already had it made up in my mind to make the custody situation official, so I went ahead and asked her if we could go ahead and make it official.

Of course she laughed it off and started telling me that'll never happen and that I think I'm better than her, etc. That part didn't faze me, but a couple days later she asked me if she could see Serenity. Now, this is something that I was willing to do, even knowing how heated the situation was because:

1. In the state of Texas the woman has full custody of the child by default.
2. Letting her see Serenity was the right thing to do.
3. Serenity greatly missed her mother and I knew she would enjoy the interaction.

So we agreed upon a location to meet and, little did I know, Nelda was about to kidnap my daughter. I arrived at the gas station first and she arrived a few minutes later. Normally, when we would meet, she would walk up to my vehicle, go straight to where Serenity was, and open the door. I've asked her numerous times to allow me to open the door, but it would only cause her to curse me out more, so I stopped asking her about it long ago. Plus this time I knew she wasn't in a good mood, so whatever. Everything happened so quickly; she walked up to the door, opened it, and picked up Serenity as if she was about to give her a big welcoming hug, and then she ran off to her vehicle. I was in shock. I didn't know if she merely wanted to get out of the hot sun, show Serenity off to her sons in her car, or what, but by the time I realized what was going on, I got out of my car and began walking to her car and as I approached—she drove off.

I began calling her and she wouldn't pick up the phone at first, but after a few minutes she began answering. She was cursing at me, telling me that I shouldn't have messed with her, that I should go ahead and take her to court if I wanted custody, that I wouldn't see Serenity until then, and all this craziness. I tried to talk her out of it and I even mentioned joint custody, but there was nothing that I could say or do to get her to let me see my daughter. There were times when I would call and seemingly get through to her and she would agree to meet me at unknown locations that, once I would get there through GPS, I found myself in the heart of the hood in a low security environment. After three or four attempts over the next couple days, I gave up and decided to go to the court house.

Shayla and I's relationship was great at the beginning, but after a few months, things became highly dysfunctional, as she began breaking up with me over minor disagreements. When Serenity's mom took her away from me that day, I was very hesitant to tell Shayla due to the close bond that she had with Serenity, but when Shayla asked about her the day after the situation—I had to let her know. That was the most painful part of our relationship. Here it is that I have my daughter, who literally just got kidnapped from me and is being held away from me, and yet my woman is calling me stupid, yelling at me, saying a real man wouldn't have allowed this to happen, and more. I tried to talk sense to Shayla, but she just took the opportunity to further chop me down. Regarding Serenity at that point, I already knew what I was about to do. I had already initiated the court process and I had to allow it to play out, but according to Shayla, I wasn't doing enough. According to her, I shouldn't have positioned myself where that could've happened and again "a real man" would take it to the streets and do what's needed to be done to get her back *even though* I couldn't prove custody to police officers when it all came down to it. I'll let you decide the best approach for yourself. Shayla and I dated for almost a year, but it was situations like that which caused us to breakup. Now many would read this part and say that breaking up was inevitable and the right thing to do and that I should be happy. But after facing all of those losses that I encountered over the years, and to get the woman or *persona* of the woman that I've been looking for in a wife at the peak of my life's experiences . . . . it was extremely difficult to let her go. Support was very important for me at that time. I was still trying my hardest to climb the ladder of success to achieve great things for my family and while doing that - I couldn't have my partner tearing me down while the world was doing the same thing.

Once again, as I was accustomed to doing, I slipped back into depression. Due to this situation, I was lost for a good two years and now that I look back on it, this means that I spent the greater part of 10 years in depression due to life's circumstances. When Shayla and I broke up, this time, I completely lost myself. I did my best to hold on, especially since Melanin Origins was in early growing stages, but it was very hard. I feel like I lost my integrity too, as I started smoking again which I hadn't done that since 2004 when I was 18 years old, but now I was 30. I say integrity because of the message that I have for young kids. I know that weed is legal in a few states in the U.S. and the diaspora of weed smokers acknowledge the benefits that it brings to many areas of life. However, I still felt that I succumbed to pressure that I should have been strong enough to champion. I also started dating multiple women at that time too. Remember, when I was in high school I had no problem in the female department, and then when I got saved in college I decided to only date women one at a time and treat them with the utmost respect. When I left college, I resumed my practice of only dating one woman at a time, but now all of that was out the window. Even though my finances weren't sent back to ground zero this time, my hopes and dreams of my perfect wife was shattered and I couldn't bare the pain. In today's age, many people date around and prescribe that life to others, but that way of life was never for me. Now that I had lost Shayla . . . . my mind changed and I no longer cared about always trying to do things the right way. I gave each woman an honest chance at some point, but, even after I knew things weren't going to work, I still entertained them for vain reasons.

I found myself in a low state once again, so I knew that I had to go to the oracle: *Frank*. I had Frank by my side right after I was fired in Florida, when I lost my job in Texas due to the DWI, and when I lost the woman I loved so dearly. Frank always listened to audiobooks and podcasts, but I wasn't into that back then. I was more into leadership books and biographies and things of that nature, but Frank told me I should read *The Alchemist* through audio book. First off, fiction wasn't my genre of reading and secondly, I never listened to an audiobook before; I preferred to read. Frank gave me the formula though. He said I could get the best results if I listened to it while I was driving to and from work, when I was cleaning at the house, or if I'm ever not doing much at the house. The interesting thing is that once I started listening, I was captivated and The Alchemist instantly became my favorite book. It actually was very much needed at that time too. The storyline is basically about a young man who is searching for his way in life and keeps finding help through guidance and wisdom from different people and situations along the way. My favorite part in the whole book is when the protagonist, named Santiago, is told by a wise man he met along his journey that the book he had been reading tells the greatest lie every told in the whole world. "What is the greatest lie?" Santiago asked. "It's this: that at a certain point in our lives, we lose control of what's happening to us, and our lives become controlled by fate. That is the world's greatest lie", said the wise man. Frank definitely pointed me in the right direction with that book, *The Power of Now*, and countless others that helped embolden me to make it easier for me to cope with all of the drastic turns that my life had taken up until that point.

Concerning Serenity—The next two months (thank God it was only two) included a bunch of detective work on my part to acquire personnel, draft legal documents, make police reports, obtain an address for her mother to be served by a deputy, and more. At the end of the whole ordeal, Nelda no showed in court after she was served by a deputy, so I won a default custody order. Physically receiving Serenity back in my home resulted in a little more detective work on my part and a few events where I was the victim of assault, but I had to go through whatever I needed to have my baby girl safe and by my side. Through all the stress, hurt, and pain... I finally got my baby girl back!

CHAPTER NINE

Of the Meaning of Progress

The idea for Melanin Origins came to me in October 2015 while I was cleaning my house. After listening to Umar and Boyce for months, a thought came to mind. I began to think about how intriguing it would be to teach my children about the theories of Booker T. Washington, W.E.B. Du Bois, & Marcus Garvey when they came of age. I couldn't wait to have discussions with them to distinguish who they would side with. I thought about how, after those discussions, we could have debates and I could challenge them to argue for sides that they disagree with, but after thinking so intensively about it for a few minutes I asked myself - "why can't I do it now?" Over the course of the next few days I took it upon myself to do research to see if what I was thinking about already existed and, sure enough, I found black history literature, but the way it was presented wasn't conducive for younger children; the concept of black inferiority was plastered all through it. Typically, when our children hear about their leaders, they hear about slavery first: slavery, fighting for equality, the civil rights movement, etc. Don't get me wrong, the struggle for freedom and equality is indeed a part of our history, but four and five year old kids don't need to know that at such early stages in their development. They just need to see people who look like them who made great accomplishments. That's exactly what they read about when it comes to Caucasians in history, so why should it be any different for my race? The way black history literature is typically presented breeds an inferiority complex in black children and superiority in others. Yet, all children simply need to know that they are great, and they should see that reflected in the literature they review.

My contention, as demonstrated through Melanin Origins, is that children need to see that they can do anything they put their mind to just like anyone else. It is paramount that this truth is reflected in their learning materials. In addition to the inferiority issue, I also noticed that our leaders were portrayed as extremely tired, old, and beaten down by life. Their pictures were typically in black and white as well. Slavery was in the content, on the cover, and everything bled with inferiority. We found that the information about black leadership was out there, but not in the form that kids needed to see it. Kids needed to see our leaders in a new, fun, and brighter way, so I did my research and decided to create a business plan in the Fall of 2015. Next, I waited until the beginning of the next calendar year, 2016, to officially form the company. Through research, Frank and I determined how to project manage the entire publishing process, we found quality editors and illustrators, we learned about the different filing entities we needed to align with, and we discovered how to fine tune the technical aspects of publishing as well. We had all this information prior to the official launch so, once January 1st came around, we were already working on the company's first book – Brick by Brick: a Snippet of The Life of Booker T. Washington, which released in April of that year. I still remember the excitement shared between my partner and me.

    With all of the business ventures that I embarked on in the past, I was never able to secure a partner or board member who genuinely took interest in the task at hand. Even though I have always been a passionate person working towards helping others, for some reason I could never convince potential allies to join me in the movement. So I was very careful in choosing people to work with when I was creating Melanin Origins. Initially, I was interested in bringing in the creatives: writers and artists I knew who simply enjoyed the craft, but after a couple months of no productivity – I decided I needed to be more strategic. Then I thought to myself . . . Frank is the one individual who I admire the most and who has been there for me during my lowest points. So I reached out to him about guiding the flow of the books I wrote and he gleefully accepted. From that point, which was in 2015, we moved forward as a team for the cause of honoring our leaders and transforming the lives of our children. On the release day of Brick by Brick, Frank and I met up with some of our old coworkers to have a celebratory drink and we were ecstatic! Everyone was so proud of our accomplishment. Frank and I boasted about the reception we were getting online and discussed our future plans for the company and when I checked my phone to show someone how to purchase the book online, there it was—*#1 New Release* on Amazon.com: the world's largest online retailer. Melanin Origins had made the best seller's list with it's very first release!!!

    There was a rush of excitement that raced through my veins! Little by little I was turning my life around and I was finding my way back into my passion. We started working our marketing strategy on social media and we got recognized by Financial Juneteenth, which is Dr. Boyce's platform. I connected with Dr. Roosevelt Mitchell & then Andre Hatchett, two of Dr. Boyce's closest associates at the time, and a few months later I was able to meet with Dr. Boyce Watkins at a speaking event in Dallas. We only had one book at that time and we initially planned on getting our first series out in a year, but that was too lofty of a goal for our first year. We were able to publish two books our first year, but in September of that year we created our curriculum for our book on Booker T. Washington. By November, we were featured in the Huffington Post! Now major platforms were beginning to recognize us. Also, in November of 2016 we released Power in My Pen: A Snippet of the Life of Ida B. Wells and our animation project *Cool Genes* was created in January 2017. The animation process was a difficult task because it was very costly, but we were able to find an awesome gentleman in Atlanta, GA willing to work with our budget. Cool Genes is the notion that every child is born with a unique ability, embedded in their DNA, to pursue excellence and be great. In February of 2017, we began our partnership with *Sickle Cell Disease Association of North Texas* leading up to the release of our book on Dr. Francis – a pioneer in treating patients with Sickle Cell Anemia. In March of that year we were featured in the Huffington Post once again, and also in the *Africa Sickle Cell News and Report.* That was major because that news platform is in Nigeria, West Africa.

After the release of our first book, people had already begun asking if we could publish their books, but we turned them down due to our own business goals for our own series.

Also, book sales weren't all that great at that time. We were putting a lot of sweat equity in on social media niche groups to get our message out, but it didn't seem to yield the results we were looking for. Well, more and more people kept requesting publishing services as time progressed, and after we turned down dozens of them, we went ahead and decided to publish others for a fee in June 2017. The next month—our first client made Amazon's Best Seller's list just like we had! A couple months later another client had done the same. We had discovered a formula for success and we found even more success and recognition after submitting our cartoon trailer to film festivals across the nation. We participated in the *Fort Worth Indie Film Showcase, Dallas Black Film Festival*, and the *Global Impact Film Festival* in Washington, D.C. While in D.C. we were featured on a panel discussion and we also won 2nd place for *Best Short Film* in Dallas!

From then on we mainly focused on publishing others which ultimately helped finance our first series and a more comprehensive curriculum. We got recognized so much that our followers topped 50k on social media, and most importantly, those followers translated to book sales and publishing contracts. Suddenly we were on dozens of podcasts and radio shows to discuss the success of Melanin Origins. I actually used all of my scheduled vacation time from work from 2016-2018 to travel to black owned bookstores throughout the nation. If I had family or friends in those cities then I would fly there and stay for a day or two with the sole purpose to make connections and get our books in stores. I did one tour in 2016; two in 2017, and 2018 was more so dedicated to out of state book festivals and networking opportunities. I was finally able to do something with my flight benefits (by now I had been working for American Airlines for five years), since prior to that I was extremely low on funds, but now I had a direct purpose for travel that was goal related.

******

From the onset of the company, Frank and I always wanted to write about pioneers who lived at least 70 years prior, so we never got into any privacy or estate issues, but towards the end of 2016 a woman reached out to us on social media regarding one of her daughters. This woman had given birth to three girls who all suffered from Sickle Cell Anemia, and one of them was a Pastry Chef who was doing amazing things for the cause. She was only 12 years old at the time, but she had her own nonprofit and she was interested in writing a book about superheroes. My heart was so touched at the resilience of this young girl and from all the toil I'm sure her mother had to endure. Unfortunately, I still had to tell her that we weren't publishing works of fiction at the moment, but if she knew of a historical pioneer that she wanted to highlight then we could work together. The mother told me she didn't even know where to begin with the process of finding that information, so I proceeded to look into it myself to help her. That's how I discovered Dr. Yvette Fay Francis-McBarnette. After a few months of dialogue with the family, we weren't able to secure a deal for the young lady to write through the company, but, by that time, I was already persuaded to tackle the topic of sickle cell, especially after I learned that it disproportionately affects people of African descent. And on top of that I wanted to display the fact that Dr. Francis was an amazing woman.

While I was writing the book and coordinating the publishing, I had some questions about her life that I wanted to get clarified, so I reached out to Dr. Francis' family to ascertain more information and let them know of the project that we had in the works. I was able to find a few social media pages of the family members and I reached out to all of them, yet I only got a response from the official Facebook Fan page of Dr. Francis. The message stated that Dr. Francis' family was already in talks with other entities about partnerships, so they chose not to work with us. We wished them well, gave them more details about our project, and even advised them to please let us know if they changed their mind, but there was no response. We moved forward. Frank and I finalized the entire process, crafted partnerships, and found our sickle cell charity of choice where we'd give 25% of all of the book's profits to aid those suffering with the disease. We began our marketing strategy with press releases and heavy social media coverage only to have one of Dr. Francis' family members openly blast our company on social media by saying, "This book is not authorized by the family of Dr. Francis and 100% of proceeds should go towards charity". That was a major blow. Mainly because we did our due diligence to reach out and advise the family of our plans for the book honoring an exemplary woman in black history, and also because I personally put my heart into this work and out of all the creative things I've done in the past . . . that project was something that I was most proud of at the time.

After doing more research on how to directly address the family, having consultations with attorneys about the right to publicity, and after forming a relationship with the husband of the late Dr. Francis, we were able to come to an agreement for the book to proceed. Interesting enough, all the controversy ensued less than three weeks prior to the release date, but I was able to hold many conversations with Mr. Olvin McBarnette (Dr. Francis' surviving husband) and even fly out to Virginia to meet him. Mr. McBarnette was actually never the source of contention, it was only a few of his children who were, but after speaking with him and stepping away from the world I was creating . . . I was able to gain an understanding into their behavior. Their mother had passed away in the Spring of 2016 and I reached out to them in the Fall of 2016. I was negligent in not providing enough time for the family to grieve. In any event, meeting Mr. Olvin McBarnette was a true blessing. He was one of the first black superintendents in the New York public schools, and he also used to work at the New York Youth Authority where he would target young men in street gangs to get them involved with positive activities in the youth center. Mr. MacBarnette was an intelligent and humble man who married a brilliant and dedicated woman; they both had six highly successful children.

After our first conversation, I already knew that this gentleman would be like a father figure to me because he lived the lifestyle that I dreamt of: a life dedicated to service, loving and marrying a woman who also was dedicated to positive change and excellence in industry, and raising six children who went on to ivy league schools and currently hold prestigious careers. That was my dream in a nutshell, so our friendship was incredible. I met him at the retirement home he was living in, we went out for dinner, and we had a great time for the one day that I was able to spend with him. Mr. McBarnette also was a World War II historian, so he even gave me a full presentation, still holding his own at 90 years of age. He and his wife were true pioneers for the American public.

******

Even though a lot of great things continued to happen on the business end, I still couldn't seem to get a hold on my personal life. I was going through a breakup with Shayla right after releasing Brick by Brick and I couldn't understand why I couldn't hold a successful relationship. I knew I had to do things differently to figure out how I could be successful in that area because it was really impacting my happiness. I needed to know how I could be the best person I could be. Eventually, I switched my gym routine from heavy lifting to more cardio and abdominal exercises. I began reading more and even getting into meditation. While I was doing my best to keep busy . . . I really didn't know what was going on with me internally. I was fighting for my confidence and it was one hell of a battle. Actually, even up until sometime in 2018, I don't know if I was ever truly confident in myself. I could always see beauty in other people, but when I looked in the mirror I always came up lacking. That is a perspective that I held onto for over a long period of time and it was clear that it was impacting me in a negative way.

The evolution of fatherhood was interesting for me back then as well. At first I was trying to have my whole family together in the same house regardless of my happiness, but that failed. I ended up getting custody of my daughter Serenity, but the relationship with my son's mother didn't work out, so now my son Uneoh couldn't be with me every day like I wanted him to. I went from a period where I was always with my son, which is what I always wanted in life, to him being 30 minutes away. I had to sneak in some time just to see him, which I'm not complaining about, but it wasn't always the easiest thing to do. I was normally working for 12-16 hours each day, Serenity was in gymnastics, and even with dealing with all that on top of other responsibilities, sometimes I would visit my son and fall asleep on his grandmother's couch. That would happen many times, so I eventually had to start taking him to the park to be active with him and make best of our time together. No doubt, however, it was surely worth it. Spending time with my children has been the highlight of my life and it also provides genuine fuel to push me forward. When it came to my son, I preferred to see him at his grandmother's house because I knew I could spend quality time with him without putting myself in compromising situations. It was a lot to juggle all by myself, especially dealing with a lack of finances, depression, maintaining my current income from my career, and building the company of my dreams. Dealing with all of this is possibly why I couldn't find success in relationships, which also played heavy on my psyche back then, negatively.

My mind frame was this: money gives leisure and I was trying to get the money to have that leisure. I wanted the leisure to better impact my family, the ability to live comfortably, and the ability to focus on creating new ideas. I was fretting heavily about my financials back then. I remember how happy I was when I got the promotion to go to Pittsburgh because I was finally able to have a comprehensive insurance plan for my children. Some people automatically qualify for government assistance and some may feel that it's a small feat to have insurance, but it was major for me to be able to do that for my kids. So all in all, supporting my children salvaged 1/3 of my monthly net income, then mortgage, bills and food, and then whatever was left over would go towards my company and my leisure

. . . which wasn't much, but that never stopped me from pursuing my goals in life.

My work at American Airlines had always been progressive though. I went from making less than 25k yearly to more than doubling that within the span of two years and tripling it in six years. Once I made it to Pittsburgh, I was promoted after a couple of months to a management position and when I transitioned back to Texas, I was promoted to assist in the training department. I already had experience with training from the work I did in Florida and in Fort Worth, but with American Airlines I found myself in a peculiar position. All of my travels and positions within the company allowed me to be the only person out of 500 people who was fluent in the major three computer systems that the company utilized. I began my work in the training department by creating presentations, presenting the material, ensuring compliance, and then I eventually transitioned to spearheading the eLearning component which was non-existent in the department until then. When I initiated the idea, I was given a team to oversee it, and we made quality learning materials. All through this time I was still networking with leaders at my job regarding dispatch and still reviewing the dispatch training information from time to time as I awaited open positions. A couple opportunities actually did arise throughout the process of time, but aircraft dispatch is such a highly coveted position that more than 500 people apply for the job within a 24 hour period. Even though I hadn't made the cut in those times to even be considered for an interview . . . I still did my best to remain hopeful and consistent.

As I progressed and as I did my best to continue to shine, I still faced common complications on the job. I remember when the NAACP made a claim of racist discrimination against

American Airlines, and I wondered how that could be. First, American is a diversity leader and wins diversity and inclusion awards nearly every year. Secondly, I always encounter a diverse set of airport employees when I travel, so I didn't understand how a blanket claim could come about based off a few isolated encounters from passengers. Even though I didn't understand the claim, I did understand the method. I always uphold the values and standards of American Airlines, because their principle and practice is better than that of our country, America, where the practice doesn't always match the principle. So with American Airlines, their principle is amazing and fair to all, but when you break it down by department heads, you're bound to find chaos if policies and procedures are not erected to ensure consistency with the overall vision. Without going into personal detail here, I'll say this was one of my major contentions while on the job, but I'm sure this strain is felt by most people of color in different industries as well. Needless to say, it was a continual strain as I did my best to champion the other areas of my life. Life on the corporate plantation can be extremely challenging at times.

Through this time, my favorite uncle, Uncle Big Boy, was living with my mother in Texas. A few years back he moved to Liberia to oversee his construction company out there and, while in Liberia, he had two near death strokes. This caused him to have other medical issues including dementia and losing different levels of body functionalities, so he needed to be cared for. Uncle Big Boy was also going through a recent divorce with his wife, so my mother took him in to care for him and tend to his needs, even while she was still working two jobs at the time in her late 50's. It was sad seeing Uncle Big Boy like that—not being able to take care of himself and not showing off his strength as he would normally do with boasting, bragging, and storytelling. Witnessing him forget where his room was was very dispiriting. I hated it and it was extremely hard for me to see him that way. I did have a lot of things going on, including my own life to clean up, but I wish I would have been able to spend more quality time with him during those years. Little did I know that his journey with us would end abruptly. I was so busy working, being depressed, trying to date and find compatibility, and running around with my kids that I guess I took his presence and spending time with him for granted. Even though I would see him a few times a month, I still felt that it wasn't enough. I had visited him plenty of times at my mother's house and in the hospital, but I took for granted that the one time that I didn't go see him was the day that he would depart from this earth. Thinking about this reminds me of a passage from The Alchemist when the wise man, Melchesidek, was telling the young boy, Santiago, about the secret to finding happiness. The story goes like this:

> *A certain shopkeeper sent his son to learn about the secret of happiness from the wisest man in the world. The lad wandered through the desert for forty days, and finally came upon a beautiful castle, high atop a mountain. It was there that the wise man lived.*
>
> *Rather than finding a saintly man though, our hero, on entering the main room of the castle, saw a hive of activity: tradesmen came and went, people were conversing in the corners, a small orchestra was playing soft music, and there was a table covered with platters of the most delicious food in that part of the world.*

The wise man conversed with everyone, and the boy had to wait for two hours before it was his turn to be given the man's attention. The wise man listened attentively to the boy's explanation of why he had come, but told him that he didn't have time just then to explain the secret of happiness.

He suggested that the boy look around the palace and return in two hours. "Meanwhile I want to ask you to do something," said the wise man, handing the boy a teaspoon that held two drops of oil. 'As you wander around, carry this spoon with you without allowing the oil to spill."

The boy began climbing and descending the many stairways of the palace, keeping his eyes fixed on the spoon. After two hours, he returned to the room where the wise man was. "Well," asked the wise man, "did you see the Persian tapestries that are hanging in my dining hall? Did you see the garden that it took the master gardener ten years to create? Did you notice the beautiful parchments in my library?"

The boy was embarrassed, and confessed that he had observed nothing. His only concern had been not to spill the oil that the wise man had entrusted to him.

"Then go back and observe the marvels of my world," said the wise man.

Relieved, the boy picked up the spoon and returned to his exploration of the palace, this time observing all of the works of art on the ceilings and the walls. He saw the gardens, the mountains all around him, the beauty of the flowers, and the taste with which everything had been selected. Upon returning to the wise man, he related in detail everything he had seen.

"But where are the drops of oil I entrusted to you?" asked the wise man. Looking down at the spoon he held, the boy saw that the oil was gone.

"Well, there is only one piece of advice I can give you." said the wisest of wise men. "The secret of happiness is to see all the marvels of the world and never to forget the drops of oil on the spoon."

The secret that I had missed greatly at this time was to experience the highs and lows of life while never taking my mind off what matters the most. Even though I felt like I was doing my best, somehow I still managed to spill the drops of oil that were on my spoon. One of my favorite people made his transition into the afterlife, and there was nothing that I could do to turn back the hands of time to be with him and share more moments with my Uncle Big Boy.

CHAPTER TEN

Of the Training of Black Men

M elanin Origins: I had lofty goals for the entire brand when we started the company. I didn't know how many books to include in the first series, but we finally decided on 10 after fluctuating from 5-7. I knew I wanted to do a series of our own that included lesser known African American pioneers, but our goals were to also add people from diverse cultures and backgrounds to the brand in the process of time as well. We planned a Latin American series, Asian series, African, etc. These were our goals for the brand, but our critics were stating we should stick with African Americans and others stated we should write about black people in different parts of the world. We also initially planned to finalize our first series within our first year of operations, which was pretty unreasonable on our part, but we were anticipating high book sales to accomplish the task. As stated in the previous chapter, scores of people were knocking at our door to publish their books, and we turned them all down until finally deciding to open the floodgates of publishing about a year later.

Again, we were branding the company as a black history book brand, but people had many fiction tales that they wanted to get published. When the requests became more frequent, we realized that publishing others would be a sure route to fund the company's projects; we decided to move forward with it. Without the necessary funds for marketing, book sales just were not making the cut at that early stage in the life of the company. Frank and I were already creating many different avenues of the company such as solidifying our charity, creating animation, account managing the bookstores, and seeking innovative technology to implement. After all that, we realized that we didn't really have to do much to "reinvent the wheel" in regards to publishing. We already had established a vast network, so, after more research, we identified that our price point and service was far better than the competitors were. We found that the marketing coaching that we provided, the illustrators that we had, and the comprehensive service we had bundled into our package made a complete difference, as other companies would charge thousands more for these services. Our competitors were nickeling and diming and they provided half of the services we provided while charging too much money.

We started publishing other authors in the Summer of 2017 and the first book under our imprint came out in Fall of that same year; the company took off from there. When the New Year came, people began contacting us left and right for our publishing services and we had over ten different publishing contracts within the first half of the year. Once we began witnessing the growth potential, we decided to continue with our initial plans of tackling our first series. We only published two books a year during our first two years in business, but, in our third year (2018) after opening the flood gates of publishing, we were able to publish the final six books to complete our first series. We were also able to finance our first comprehensive curriculum supplement for the series as well. So the foundation for Melanin Origins was laid.

Speaking of foundation laying, I am reminded of the story Booker T. Washington told about erecting Tuskegee Institute with his students. The very first few attempts were not successful at all. On the first attempt, Booker and his students made over 20k bricks but, since he was new to the craft, the bricks were not made correctly. Therefore, when Booker T. attempted to build with them, he failed. Imagine that—so much labor and effort gone in vain not to mention money that was spent as well. At that time he still didn't have steady revenue to fund the vision he had for the school neither did he know where the money would come from. Booker then hustled up more money to attempt making more bricks, and after several more failed attempts he finally got it down and his students got to work. Not only were they able to make good bricks to support the foundation of new school buildings, but Booker T. Washington and his students also began selling bricks, which added a new revenue stream to financially support the school. It was a win, win for all parties involved. This relates to the process whereby we created revenue streams through Melanin Origins, so while laying the foundation for the company I was also able to determine the proper branding / messaging for other avenues of the company.

We had our ups and down, but it never deterred us from our goals. For instance, we learned about the right to publicity though the Dr. Francis situation. That was a major personal lesson for me because I've seen that my heart can sometimes be bigger than my head. Often times I want to do so much to help, not realizing that it may jeopardize other things that I'm working on. Luckily for me, consultations with lawyers, sheer humility, and the kind heart of Mr. Olvin McBarnette was able to save the day in that case.

******

When Melanin Origins first began, we wanted to have an all-black staff of freelancers and contractors, but we found that that was pretty difficult due to the cost of living in America. Therefore, we eventually decided to global source our projects and we ended up finding a diverse set of quality illustrators throughout the world who were able to go far above and beyond our requests. At first we actually had one illustrator to rely on, but when the work started ramping up, plenty of other illustrators began reaching out to us at the price points we were interested in. The universe was bending to our will and bringing about the things that we desired directly to our doorstep. As we grew, we were able to allocate time to learn more about the processes to where we could cut out the middle man and save more money. That allowed us to get smarter about our finances and grow even more in the industry.

In the early stages, our goal was simply to sell books at local events (vend) once or twice a month at high traffic locations. This was a part of our process of building awareness for the community and in securing sales. We were doing what we could on social media and we were making great headway there, but we also felt the need to focus on our community at physical locations as well. Even though our company's leadership was based in the Dallas-Fort Worth area, we still desired to break into the D.C., Chicago, Atlanta, and other markets as well. Frank and I believed in our products and services and we also found that when we were face to face with our audience, they greatly adored us as well. We learned that it was only a matter of presenting ourselves to our audience to get the sales we desired.

The mission of Melanin Origins is to provide quality educational materials which inspire young minds to aspire for excellence while embracing their heritage. Our vision is to become the largest culturally competent book provider in the United States of America.

We tell the story right and we have some of the best illustrators in the industry. Our stories are inspirational and it encourages children to accomplish the same things that our leaders did. There's a moral in each story and not only that, we don't always follow the mode of introducing conflict especially given the nature of the content. Most importantly, we combat the notion of black inferiority with our literature. While trying to find black history books relevant for my children who were one and two years old before creating Melanin Origins, I discovered that over half of black history books and literature for children are created by people who are not of African descent. I found that many of the people who created the books were not able to provide an accurate portrayal of the black experience in America. Also, some of the information is extremely bland and unappealing. It usually has black and white pictures with a storyline of someone from 1805 – 1862 explaining "so and so" did this, and it repeats this process over and over again when you flip through the pages. Lastly, and most importantly for African-Americans, all of the information breeds the notions of slavery, civil rights, and struggle upon struggle. The derogatory experiences that black people have experienced in America and around the world are needed for children of the appropriate age, but Melanin Origins contends that that harsh reality is not conducive to a healthy psyche for three, four, and five year old children. Since information about our leaders was not available for children in First Grade and below, Melanin Origins decided to step in and fill that void with stories of leadership, empowerment, STEM, great achievement, and by making it fun in the process! This is how we began the process of the training of black men and women. Start while young.

In so many ways our kids are being told that they need to assimilate, that they're inferior, and that the natural aspects about them are uncomely or inheritably deficient. All this comes back to a reflection on their skin color. Melanin Origins contends that we need for our children to embrace everything about themselves and focus on excellence, because excellence is what provides for true culture.

As stated previously, our vision is to become the largest culturally competent publishing company, and that is carried out through vertical and horizontal growth. Vertical growth involves taking the stories that we've done for our first series of African American pioneers and telling those same stories to older age groups while providing more details and adequate verbiage conducive to the age and development stages. Horizontal growth involves expanding our books to other people groups such as Latin America, Asia, Africa, and other lands. We'll tell the stories of lesser known pioneers and engage the children of those various cultures with stories of hope as well.

One thing that is clear is that Culturally Relevant Pedagogy is the best way to reach and engage children concerning education. Seeing people who look like them represented in literature and being taught in ways that provides a culturally relevant understanding, is a sure-fire way to spark a light bulb in a child's brain. Black children in

America have many negative media outlets as is from the continued stories of racial discrimination and police brutality on the news down to our own genre of music which also doesn't always paint us in a positive light. Imagine what would happen to a young black child if they began to be inundated with culturally relevant teachings that displayed how African-Americans in the late 1800's and early 1900's were making great strides in different industries even during those times? It would really help knowing that these pioneers were doing more than singing, rapping, acting, or playing sports.

The sum total of my learning led me to believe that the media has the story all wrong about people who look like me and that the educational system has the wrong idea of how to educate people who look like me. I learned about the need for Culturally Responsive Pedagogy. According to Brown University, Culture is central to learning. It plays a critical role, not only in communicating and receiving information, but also in shaping the thinking process of groups and individuals. Culturally Responsive Teaching is a pedagogy that acknowledges, responds to, and celebrates fundamental cultures and offers full, equitable access to education for students from all cultures. It is a pedagogy that recognizes the importance of including students' cultural references in all aspects of learning.

After stumbling upon this information, I finally understood the necessity for white supremacy to perpetuate stories in the media about negative experiences regarding African-Americans. I understood why African-Americans have the only genre of music that celebrates the disrespect of women, the disregard for black family, the killing of black people, the usage and distribution of drugs, and all other forms of criminality. It finally became evident to me why it was absolutely necessary for young black kids to be introduced to their historical leaders with the notion of slavery, civil rights, and struggle. As a country, we have been practicing Culturally Responsive Pedagogy in reverse, and this is what is needed for the notion of white supremacy and racism to thrive. Even President Barack Hussein Obama was ridiculed and disrespected practically every day of his presidency, but Melanin Origins, LLC has discovered the remedy.

It is of primary importance that Black Americans rear a generation (generations) of children who fully comprehend the greatness that lies within. Children who will not be swayed by the negativity perpetuated by the media, white supremacy, or similar brothers and sisters who are still in lost in the "sunken place". The position of Melanin Origins is this: changes need to be made, primarily through education in the school system, and at home. This is why we have created Black History Books for kids that do not solely focus on slavery. This is why, as Black Owned Publishers, our leadership decided to turn our historical leaders into children so that they can relate to the child audience. This is why we began by targeting children in First Grade and below so that we can reach them with message of greatness and achievement from actual people who look like them. We want them to realize that black people achieved magnificent things during a time where blacks weren't even considered human by some standards.

Culturally Responsive Pedagogy is the wave of the future and it will provide hope for the black community in America and throughout the world. With a diehard focus on a culturally relatable education, making it a habit to have family dialogues on excellence, and encouraging our young people that they have everything within them to accomplish their dreams - we can witness a change in our households, in our neighborhoods, our communities, and then the workforce. This will spread through every aspect of the educational and governmental system at large.

When we initially conducted our research for starting Melanin Origins, we found 1 in 5 of U.S. students will not complete high school on time and earn a diploma. Furthermore, 1 in 5 adults in North Texas cannot read. Now, Dallas-Fort Worth is the hub of North Texas, so I took that personally. Through all of our findings it became clear to us that people of color in every major U.S. city are in need of literacy assistance the most. If we want to succeed in having better communities, better race relations, lower crime rates, ingenuity in the inner city, a generation of people that replaces trap culture with innovative excellence as the new dominant norm, etc. then we must be able to find the most effective ways to reach people of color.

A 2018 report conducted by Literacy Instruction For Texas stated that Dallas' population is expected to grow by over one million people in the next 20 years and the illiteracy rate is projected to grow faster than the population rate. As the clock keeps ticking and our nation becomes more illiterate, we must recognize that our babies are growing at the same time. Our nation must come to understand the potency and impact of culturally responsive pedagogy.

Here's a Christian perspective regarding the need for culturally responsive pedagogy through the eyes of Pastor Tony Evans:

> *"Growing up in urban America during the Civil Rights Era in a Christian context of racism, segregation and an incomplete historical education didn't give me an opportunity to know who I really*

was. In my all-black classrooms, I learned about white culture and white history. I read about Paul Revere and his midnight ride. But what my teachers failed to mention was that on the night of Paul Revere's ride, another man—a black man— Wentworth Cheswell also rode on behalf of our nation's security. He rode north with the same exact message. Without an authentic self-awareness, African-Americans often struggle as we seek to play on the same team toward the same goal in the body of Christ. But just as relevant is the need for awareness among my white brothers and sisters concerning who we are, and who God has created and positioned us to be at this critical time in our world."

Dr. Evans refers to the body of Christ here, but I extend this concept to the nation at large. I believe we all desire to play on the same team even as American citizens desiring life, liberty, and the pursuit of happiness.

******

I made a conscious decision a few years ago to listen to audiobooks and podcasts in the morning instead of the radio. Transitioning to wholly positive messages in the morning has made a significant impact on my daily experience on the job, in my interactions throughout the day, and in my personal life as well. Every morning I alternate from T.D. Jakes, Les Brown, Infinite Waters (Ralph Smart), The Tony Robbins podcast, and other "Law of Attraction" motivational coaches. The Tony Robbins podcast is one of my favorites to listen to though because Tony is an outstanding individual, motivator, and coach! He also is a multi-millionaire who has fellow multi-millionaire and billionaire guests on his show who all share snippets of their success story while dropping nuggets on how to attain similar success. I noticed a trend while listening to his show where most guests state that they do not watch the news. They say that they understand that the news is geared to attack your psyche with primarily negative stories from around the world and your psyche, as Tony Robbins puts it, is also not always prone to ensure your best benefit either. Your brain will take past disappointments and failures, the anxieties of the future, and current day ills and exploit them. This is what causes depression, mediocrity, anger, and it is also what causes many negative behaviors leading up to suicide. Furthermore, every episode of the Tony Robbins Podcast ends with this statement, "success is 80% psychology and 20% mechanics". Tony advocates that if we can work hard enough to train our psyche for success then all else will follow.

I will say that it is definitely a privilege for certain individuals to not watch the news or be affected by the negative stories covered therein. When I worked as a Juvenile Supervision Officer, it was common practice to not show the local news on the television. Why? Because if a child in our facility seen something bad happen in his neighborhood . . . it could have a very detrimental impact on him or her and the security of the facility. They could want to fight, they might become depressed, they could desperately want to escape, or they might even want to take their own lives. Yes . . . it's that serious and with that being said, I understand why we have multi-millionaires sharing how they refuse to allow the ills of the world infiltrate their psyche as well.

Is it possible that black people in America can attain the same results of happiness and success by simply not following the news? That's definitely something to ponder. Every day, somewhere in America, there is a negative story being ran about racist hate crimes, inequitable court rulings, discrimination in housing or education, the degradation of our neighborhoods and communities, and also the stories of us killing our own selves (which we must put forth even greater effort in addressing and combating). All around us there is negativity, so how can we choose to ignore it? How can I smile and entertain nonsensical conversations at a work cocktail party while there is a full-fledged onslaught against the Trayvon Martin's of the world and other young people who look just like me. . . HOW???

Now, this is not a question that I propose to Tony or his pals . . . it's just something I'm saying to get you to consider what I'm about to say next. Tony's remedy is this—he says, "At the same time that there are negative things happening in the world, there also are equally as much positive things happening as well." Will we choose to succumb to fear, depression, and hopelessness or will we stand up and choose to use it as fuel for motivation, happiness, and championing the one thing it appears society is out to destroy—the black community. When a student drops out, another graduates. When a child loses his life, a baby is born. When an African-American is discriminated against, another civil rights attorney wins a landmark case. Every day great things are happening, and now it is about time that we, as a collective group of people, learn how to train our mind and bodies to FOCUS!

Two Key Areas of Focus:

First, we must focus on living in the present. Our brain creates mental movies for us to reflect on the past and project the future. This can be good and/or bad, but most importantly . . . it's not reality. What is real is that you are reading these words right now, and that you are breathing and that you have the ability to look around and be thankful for the opportunity to enjoy this current moment. That is your choice. The past cannot be changed, but what can you do to ensure a better future? It's normal and extremely easy to get anxiety while projecting into the future, but why allow it to negatively affect you when you know that you are doing what needs to be done TODAY?

The second key area of focus is in placing a greater emphasis on the "how" and not the "what". I can't speak for everyone, but I know that I am an expert at the "what". As soon as I hear someone tout something offensive I say, "What!? What'd you say?" When I was young, if someone expressed a problem with me, I'd say, "What!? What's up?" There's a person I know—he's a deranged individual who disrespects women, places proclaimed hate group leaders in political office, calls African-Americans "The blacks", has school yard disputes with respected community leaders, orders travel bans on the basis of religion, breaks up families with no regard on the basis of "immigration", and embodies everything that represents prejudice. This individual became the 45th President of the United States and certain people have the audacity to defend him . . . "What!? What do you mean?" Yes, it's very easy to get lost in the "what". African Americans from all social classes can expound on the ills that they face along with the historical oppression perpetrated by white supremacy that has been destroying us for generations.

We are very familiar with the "what", but in order to transition from merely knowing about it and understanding how we were, and are still, impacted by such things—we must put our feet down and get to work on the "how", which is the application of what we know (wisdom).

Wisdom is the principle thing, therefore get wisdom! There will be many more "What!?" moments to come, but I believe the best way to move forward is for each of us to perfect the "how". How am I supposed to respond? How can I better myself? How should I address this individual or situation? How can I best appreciate God's blessings in my life today? How can I safely make it home or out of this situation? How can I ensure a better future for my children? How can I not repeat the same cycle of my parents? How can I not become totally victimized by societal pressures and limitations? How? We must train our psyches to strongly consider the "how" over the "what". By doing so, we will be better positioning ourselves to have a healthy psyche that will be more apt to enjoy the present moment. Forward thinking progressives is what we must be if we want to witness a change in our lives and in our communities.

I fully understand that some readers might already be practicing this, but to you—I'd like to encourage you to impart this wisdom to another. Some readers might catch the notion of personal responsibility sprinkled throughout this thread, and might even draw assimilationist conclusions as well. To you—I'd say that the notion of assimilation is far from the values of Melanin Origins LLC. We advocate psychological health, understanding threatening and opposing dynamics, educational excellence, community building, and individualistic direct action that benefits the collective. At the same time that we support civil rights attorneys who champion our causes, we also support each individual person and encourage them to believe in themselves, because God has great things in store for their lives. We must protect our psychological health at all costs. If that means detoxing from the news then so be it. If that means not entertaining controversial conversations, then so be it. While negative things are happening, equally positive things are taking place as well. We need to be able to feel the pain of our own personal struggle, for those in worse positions in the struggle, and we also need to formulate a collective or individual plan about what we are going to do about it. We have the power within us to drastically change our own reality and that of another through perfecting the "how" through the application of wisdom.

******

Depression: I've sunk down to the bottom of the sea;
I'm standing in the battle field with no weapon.
Deep in the trenches. It's like I've seemed to barely
make the team, but I'm still sitting on the bench.
With no compensation, just eager determination.
Minus procrastination, because opportunity's
waiting.
I can't take it, hell no! I can't face it. My life – I'll
take it, if it's a game then I ain't playing with
depression.
You see my eyes cried tears that should be tatted
cause I thought Jesus had my back.
I'm in the depths of despair, there's no one left that
even cares, I can't tell moms because I already put
those grays in her hair.

This air I breathe is a joke, I'm better off blowing smoke, because I'm poison, all my talking is just noise.

Depression — the closest kin to suicide, but family means nothing when you're ready to die.

Where was my family when then they took away my piece of the pie.

No words of comfort, no letters hope, not even a "Hi, hey, hello, how're you doing . . . can I lend you a hand."

I've been shot in both knees, how you expect me to stand? Depression: you're born alone, you die alone understand.

But let me stop rhyming, cause this is not even poetry.

These are the cries of a man facing a dream deferred.

A deter turned dead end, rebirth turned hell-bent; a curse that descended out of the mouth of the Lord!

So now I can't talk to God about my problems... I can't turn to my family...

All I can do is face this depression. The closest kin to suicide, so today, I accept my fate Lord - I'm ready to die.

Even though I wrote that piece during times in my depths of depression while facing the DWI issue . . . I still would rehearse those words from time to time throughout the years. It was the only way that I had to express myself, and I was the only person that I could relay the message to. I learned the hard way that the women I dated didn't want to hear any of the struggles or battles I had. Also, way too many people relied on me or held me at such high esteem, so allowing them into the inner workings of Louie would have tarnished relationships, added strain, or even caused their perception of me to be altered. Consequently, I kept it all to myself for the most part. I had counselor friends who I would speak to, but I never established a true professional relationship out of not wanting to lose the friendship. I believe the main cause of my depression was because I still felt as if I wasn't experiencing the results that I desired in life. After having so many great intentions and accomplishing so many things in the name of the community, I still found myself in heavy financial strain and alone most of the time. On numerous occasions, I felt as if doing right did not matter and nothing that I could do would help me live a more fulfilled life. Yes, I was falsely accused and fired from my first job, yes I got the DWI and lost my entire career field and everything I'd worked for, yes, I had two kids back to back out of wedlock, and yes I did suffer mentally, emotionally, and financially from it all. Looking back on not having a father in the house to teach me the things I needed to learn and to help steer me in the right direction was constantly embedded in my mind too. All I could do was dwell on the negativity of the past, feel the present pain, and fret about the future.

As I previously mentioned before, what I learned from Tony Robbins and others is that when negative things are happening, equally positive things are taking place all around us at the same time. So through it all, I was able to have moments of triumph and victory. I was able to see the Hand of God through my children, through promotions, through incredible ideas and support from people in the community, and through individuals telling me that I inspire them and the work that I'm doing gives them hope. I eventually got my first house, and I accomplished most of my goals for the company. I think the depression sunk in more by thinking about the way things would have been if I didn't make so many mistakes in my past. Each successful venture that I was experiencing would've been that much better. I would have been in a better financial situation to have the experience I wanted in relationships and I would have been in a better position to invest more in the things I was interested in. I wanted to witness monumental deeds so that the company could have a better turn around and I wouldn't have had to spend 12-18 hour days each day toiling on business and startup ideas. My life just didn't appear to be the way how I thought it would be. It's interesting how I was trapped in my own mind for so long, and again, it actually wasn't until the writing of this book that I realized that I had battled with the demon of depression for over a period of 10 years! Many highs and many lows, but when I was down . . . I was down hard.

All that changed in the spring of 2018 however. Not just because I made the declaration, but after reading so many books: *The Alchemist, The Power Of Now, The Compound Effect, Up from Slavery, The Soul of Black Folks, and The Philosophy and Opinions Of Marcus Garvey, and to top it off - The Secret* . . . I found a new found hope. My entire worldview was altered and I was refreshed. Up from Slavery was a choice favorite—Booker T. reminded me that the things that I was doing to be successful is what he did. Humility, meekness, trying my best, working hard and even as I reflected on my personal life . . . Booker held excellence as the standard. He taught me that even if you fall short, you can always find your way back. Booker also showed me how everything that he did was for black people. Even though certain people of his own race ridiculed him and wrote him off as an "Uncle Tom", all of the work that he did went to directly benefit the members of his own race. Booker T. Washington reminded me of what hard work looked like and, even though each day might not be as pretty as you hoped, you can still rest content that you have done your due diligence; I learned that I can have faith that the work I was doing will pay off. Hell, Booker got the equivalent of millions of dollars from Caucasians to do work for black people. These were industry leaders, some were racists, some ex-slave masters, etc., but he saw the good in everyone and did what was necessary to positively affect the people who he needed to impact.

So *Up From Slavery* still remains one of my favorite books (after *The Alchemist*). *The Secret* also brought about a discovery in my life, as my cousin Ivor has made himself into a major success and he credits it to this very same book. Not too long ago, Ivor would meet up with Aydn and I at Aydn's place as we discussed our business plans. I remember one time I was at Aydn's place in the beginning of my M.O. days and we were discussing Ivor's success. Ivor also joined us and that's when he mentioned a book that discussed the law of attraction. Aydn happened to have the book, so they both highly recommended that I read it and digest the content for myself. At this time, I was already working on many projects and reading other literature that pertained specifically to my industry, but after witnessing the growth of Ivor . . . I knew I had to read it for myself. Ivor went from having a piano business with one school district, to working in a pharmacy, to owning his own and now multiple pharmacies. Once he established himself financially, which all seemed to happen very swiftly, he then began working on his passion projects of producing music and films in Hollywood. This greatly inspired me and to hear him credit his success to a book . . . I was greatly inclined to learn more about this.

What is the secret? That's exactly what I was itching to know when I opened the book, but after a few pages it tells you clearly. The secret is *the law of attraction.* The law of attraction is never spelled out in the Bible which I'm used to reading, but the Bible does make reference to certain things like, seek and ye shall find, and how having faith of a mustard seed will cause you to move mountains, that life and death are in the power of the tongue, etc., but it never dives deep into the inner workings. It doesn't provide detail about this great spiritual universe that God placed us in and, while the Bible makes mention of humans having dominion, it doesn't scientifically show how this works and how we can use it to our advantage. That's what the law of attraction teachings seemingly breakdown. The Secret explains that there is spirit energy throughout the whole universe, and when we make positive affirmations—we then release frequencies into the universe and we attract the things that we speak and believe in to ourselves. We bring it into our lives even as a magnet attracts metal to itself. The Secret provides excerpts from wealthy individuals, founding fathers, major world pioneers, and some of the most creative business leaders and they all harp on the same things—belief in one's self is paramount and speaking those things through positive affirmation causes supernatural manifestation. I had found that in many cases we have been taught to do, to be, to try, and to work, but what hasn't been fully revealed is the supernatural ability that each individual has to create their own reality and the role that the entire universe plays in bringing it into fruition. Learning these things brought about a major change in my attitude and behavior.

I became reminded of who I AM, which was instilled in me once I got saved. The book reminded me of where God placed me and the gifts and abilities he gave me when he gave me dominion and I've never been the same since. "As a man thinketh in his heart so is he", "confess with your mouth and it shall be", "Abraham believed God and it was accounted to him for righteousness". I came to realize that happiness and the realization of any goal all boils down to our belief and faith. When we continuously speak on and envision the things that we desire, that determines our path. It helps us make up our mind, and it helps us release frequencies out into the universe which attracts the things to us, and that is how I forever got myself out of depression. I began affirming love for myself. I started affirming gratitude towards God and all that he has given to me. I began to focus on contentment while never remaining complacent. I found that this is the key for happiness. I learned that obstacles may come my way, but it's simply a distraction and that by standing tall and holding true to the fact that "All things work together for good for those who love God and are the called according to His purpose". . . I now know that I can continue to my final destination with more ease and finesse. With this new piece of information I was renewed in spirit, further emboldened to pursue my aspirations with Melanin Origins, and all the more prepared to have the black family unit that I've always dreamed of.

CHAPTER ELEVEN

Making Their Beds
So They Can Lie In Them

In 2016, I began following Dr. Boyce Watkins & Dr. Umar Johnson on social media pretty heavily. At the time, the national climate was ripe with police killings of unarmed black men, racist rants against then President Barack Obama, and the 2016 elections were soon to take place with the most bigoted bully to ever be candidate: #45. It felt as if African-Americans, in masse, were beginning to witness and experience more racism than they've ever undergone in our generation. All of the closet racists were coming out and spewing their hatred with boldness and no consequence. During all of this, Dr. Umar was in a position to share his knowledge and motivate our race to unify and learn more about history so that we can be better equipped to combat the evil that has been seeking our destruction for generations. Dr. Boyce Watkins also rose to prominence in that time as well, as he harped on financial literacy and the power of owning your own business.

One of the chief topics Dr. Boyce would discuss was that of Black Wall Street in Tulsa, Oklahoma. His M.O. was to highlight the success and business mindset the people had in that thriving community. Even though the town was destroyed by angry white mobs, he wanted to show how black economics can thrive and how we can better position ourselves in society. So both of these gentlemen referred to a better future by highlighting or making note of the past, and that was my greatest inspiration at the time. Actually, the national climate and the rise of these two gentlemen is the reason why Melanin Origins was created in the first place. Not to mention that I already had fell-out with my classmates from PCC, many of whom went on to be police officers.

In my humble opinion, President Barack Obama excelled in his craft and gracefully represented all Americans, but, according to his detractors, there was nothing that he could do right. Ever since he announced his run for presidency in 2007, he was inundated with racist verbal assaults. A few years later, a young man named Trayvon Martin was killed in 2012 by a neighborhood watchman and that unjustified killing sparked a national debate. Now, these types of unjustified killings of unarmed black men have been happening all across the country for ages, but due to new technological breakthroughs such as smart phones, we've been able to capture some of the events and stories that have been continuously plaguing our communities. News travels a lot faster now, so hearing about police killings started to become more rampant. At the same time that blacks were getting gunned down for running away from the police, holding cell phones in their hands or resisting arrest unarmed, the lives of Caucasian males would be spared even when actively attacking police officers with weapons. As seen in the cases of Eric Garner and Alton Sterling, African American would even get murdered for simply for passively resisting arrest for selling cigarettes or CD's on street corners.

Black people had gotten to a point where we began to excel in the industry. We were excelling so tremendously that it showed us that we could even become President. This expansion of greatness in the black community caused white supremacy to boil up like a volcano; it tapped into something black people hadn't overtly and consistently witnessed since the 1960s. Great displays of racist acts of aggression began to lead to the deaths of our young men and women, and all of this led to the rise of great individuals such as Boyce & Umar.

What my Caucasian friends didn't understand about this whole dilemma was that it's clear that the suspect's actions are not always the cause of his death. Professors and business men alike have experienced police brutality and unjust jailing, and what my Caucasian counterparts seemed not to comprehend is that *I* too could easily become a victim any day even while I'm making my best attempt to be the best representative I can be for my community. This is when I began getting closer to the sentiments of Pan Africanism through Dr. Umar: the concept that what's done *for* black people must be done *by* black people. The notion that we have to be the ones looking out for our own and taking care of ourselves, because clearly that's where we are safest. So with all this, and learning about Booker T., it made me feel obligated to join the struggle for liberation.

Booker T. Washington was called to lead a school in Tuskegee, Alabama, but the classroom was in an old hen house: small and uncomfortable. He had a great vision for what the learning environment should be and he thought his students deserved excellence, so he did everything he could to provide that for them. Self-determination was Booker's claim to fame. He was born a slave then freed at a young age through the Emancipation Proclamation and, in the process of time, he traveled over 500 miles, often by foot, so that he could go to school. Throughout that entire time he didn't have money to travel or attend school. Once he arrived in Hampton, Virginia he slept on and under sidewalks, he worked small odd jobs, yet his primary goal was to be accepted in school, of which, he had no money to attend. He would greet the teachers and administrators each day with a smile, asking if he could help clean or do anything he could to work for his education. After being denied many times and after living many homeless nights, he was finally given an opportunity to clean one of the residence buildings, and he did so well that he got hired on the spot. The funds he received wasn't enough for school, so he had to work overtime and at other jobs just so he could remain in school. He had 16-20 hour days, many days. He did what he had to do and when he graduated, he went back to his hometown to educate former slaves (his people).

After doing a great job leading in his hometown, he was called to Tuskegee Institute where he thrived even more. Now, those who study Booker T. may know him for his Atlanta Compromise. Some love him for this and some despise him for it, but you can judge it how you see it. The Atlanta Compromise basically said, to an audience of white and black people, that Blacks will focus on educating themselves, taking jobs that will help boost their local economies in their neighborhoods and support their families, and, as they took time to excel in those areas, blacks wouldn't be too concerned with the political process of voting. Booker's thought process was that blacks had just came out of slavery a few years ago, and there were still many acts of aggression against blacks perpetrated by whites in the south, especially as it pertained to the political process. So Booker decided to, in one swipe, empower blacks with an opportunity to grow and create within their own space without the fear of white aggression and appease white people by advocating that blacks will hold off on political agitation or entry into the political process for the time being. He felt that whites would see the progress that blacks would make on their own and then become overwhelmingly convinced that suffrage would be beneficial for everyone. That was Booker T's ideology and what he became mostly known for outside of the outstanding work that he was doing at Tuskegee. There were some who clung to his words and hailed him as a savior like figure among the black race, but many, especially in the north looked down upon Booker and this "compromise".

Booker's worldview: He would say, "Look at how we are improving, and the steps we're making towards progressing towards the American Dream. We hear people calling for political actions and what not, but if we were to aggressively fight for those things then we would be met with a lot of aggression, and you can already see how often we're getting lynched and killed in the street as is. If we can only focus on sharpening ourselves up, getting an industrial education, and stimulating our own economy—then we can find stability and peace among our own, and we won't have problems with vigilante groups." His detractors seen it a different way though. "He's saying I shouldn't vote? Ain't I a man? Aren't these my God given rights even as a citizen of this country?" "Whites will disadvantage me with their vote . . . why should I let this happen."

Booker's main detractor was an individual from his own race: W.E.B. Du Bois. He was from a small town in

Massachusetts (the North), but Booker was from Virginia (the South), and moved to West Virginia. Both of them had parents of each race: a slave mother and a slave master father whom they did not have much contact with, but, being from the north, Du Bois was able to experience greater privilege than someone who was born a slave. He could look white people in the face and he could hold conversations and have disagreements, whereas in the south, even young boys would be killed out of mere jealousy for simply looking at a white woman, as demonstrated in the life and death of Emmett Till. Whites in the south could do all types of crimes against blacks with immunity. Actually, Ida B. Wells documented, while on her anti-lynching campaigns, that over 3,400 people had been lynched over a three year period (1889-1922) and two-thirds of that figure were black men. Du Bois, however, felt much empowered to say as he felt and fight for the things that he believed should be fought for without the direct, imminent threat that was faced in the south. So he created the talented tenth – a concept that emphasized the necessity for higher education to develop the leadership capacity among the most able 10 percent of black Americans.

Du Bois also cofounded the NAACP – the National Association for the Advancement of Colored People whose mission is to ensure the political, educational, social, and economic equality of rights of all persons and to eliminate race-based discrimination. Furthermore, he became heavily involved in the process of fighting for equal rights for blacks even if it meant protesting in the streets, legal advocacy, propaganda, or whatever it would take. Now, I love Dr. Du Bois, but I do have a slight issue with him. The problem I have is that I don't like black leaders publically opposing each other. A debate is one thing, and a passionate one is even better, but Du Bois openly challenged Booker T. Washington many times.

He called him out by name in his book (actually named an entire chapter after him), wrote about him in news articles, and made greater attempts to rally blacks against Booker and his ideology. Booker, however, never actually addressed or made mention of his detractors . . . even the white ones.

Not only did Du Bois have a problem with Booker T., but he also had a problem with Marcus Garvey who was considered the "Provincial President of Africa". Garvey was a young man from Jamaica who had a powerful message of *Africa for the Africans!* He began his career as an apprentice for a printing press and traveled throughout the Caribbean and Central America. During his apprenticeship Garvey noticed that, everywhere he traveled, black people were at the lowest levels of industry, often unpaid, and doing the most work while stimulating economies for a white elite class. Everywhere he turned he witnessed diligent black laborers doing the toil, but fairer skinned individuals were reaping the benefits of that labor. He found an issue that this was happening everywhere he turned, and that is what provided fuel for his powerful message of Africa for the Africans. Garvey would say, "Black people, we have a home continent and we need to rise from where we are to go free that continent. There are so many talented and skilled black people spread across the globe... surely we can take our skills back to Africa and rebuild it to best fit our needs where we won't be subjugated as we are." Many don't know, but Marcus Garvey had the largest black movement in history up until the civil rights movement yet he is blotted out of the history books in public schools. Why would such a great leader who accomplished so many things and who led one of the largest, historical, non-violent movements not be taught to the masses in public schools nationwide?

Garvey created an international shipping company, a newspaper that was in circulation with over 250k subscribers (imagine that in the early 1900's), he created the Universal Negro Improvement Association which was dedicated to racial pride, economic self-sufficiency, and the formation of an independent black nation in Africa. His message was one of power and strength to the black man in America who has been having his life and sense of worth sucked out of him, yet, all Du Bois could do was publically oppose and tear him down as well. While Garvey was advocating for blacks to "do for self", Du Bois was suggesting a more integrative experience of which he believed was the best way forward. He was not interested, at the time, in going back or shipping all blacks back to Africa. Now, Garvey's contention was that blacks would never be able to achieve total equality and equity in America. Individual blacks would achieve a certain level of success and it may appear that all others could accomplish the same, but, Garvey believed, so long as prejudice exists and so long as competition is prevalent . . . there will always be an underclass of whites who will either act as a vigilante mob or systematically oppress blacks. Even though we will see some strides, as a whole we will not be able to attain what we want due to certain factors, namely a bigoted, white supremacist group amongst white people who will always be allowed to have their way. Take the Ku Klux Klan (KKK), for example, who meet in the woods and other underground channels and conduct acts of aggression against colored people while wearing masks. When they take the masks off, they return to their posts as civic employees, police officers, judges, teachers, etc.

Ironically, after the U.S. government convicted Garvey of mail fraud and deported him out of the country, Du Bois eventually converted to Pan Africanism and even moved to Ghana where he died and was buried.

I learned about Marcus Garvey when I was 24 years old when one of my ex-coworkers, Said, turned me on to him. Yes, my brother Said Muhammad from Tarrant County Juvenile. When I met Said I had just came back from Florida, and I was "holier than thou" when it came to Christianity. For some reason however, I never witnessed to him in an attempt to convert him or persuade him for Christ. I'm not sure if it was because I didn't want to bring that energy to work or if it was the fact that I was always impressed when I heard him speak that I was too intimidated to question his knowledge. The thing is, Said wasn't trying to convert anyone either, or, at least not to religion. Said was constantly finding bright ways to convert young men who have lost their way to a more positive lifestyle and he was a beast with it! After serving our country, Said was a counselor in the federal prison prior to finding employment at Tarrant County Juvenile. When he spoke, everybody listened. One thing that everyone knew about Said is that he really loved music, and he actually gave me a few CDs to listen to at times. Musiq Soulchild, the Isley Brothers, Ludacris, and a few more, but the one that stood out the most to me was a rap group called Dead Prez. I remember listening to their "Cut Off The Radio" album, but I was stuck on one song "Malcolm, Garvey, Huey". So the next time I saw Said, I asked him: "Who were the people that Dead Prez were talking about in their song? And that's the day Said taught me about Marcus Garvey and Huey P. Newton (of course I knew who Malcolm X was). From the time I heard of the things Garvey stood for, I was determined to know more. Interesting enough, I learned about Ida B. Wells shortly after that by hearing her name in a Kanye West song and then again a few years later while watching a television show called The Wire, but I digress.

Booker T., Du Bois, and Garvey laid out three progressive strategies for black people living in America.

Booker T.: self-determination, self-reliance. Let's get these industrial skills, let's build for ourselves so we can do for ourselves and prove ourselves as equals. And let's do the best we can. When you see white people—smile, shake their hand, and greet them.

Du Bois: political action now, access to higher education, and we're taking it to the streets to protest if we need to. We need to get this right now. We're going to put it in their face and we're going to demand it.

Garvey: his is the least spoken of regarding black people in America which, in my humble opinion, is a shame. How long will we sit back and watch our own people get destroyed in countries that don't respect us as equals? Thinking – is it going to happen to me next? When is it going to come to my family? Marcus Garvey calls all talented and skilled blacks in the diaspora to take their talents to Africa. The world has fallen in love with the fictional country Wakanda from the Black Panther movie, but no one is seeking to build a real life Wakanda in any place in the world. Nevertheless, Garvey preached self-determination as well as Pan Africanism, again—what is to be done for black people must be done by black people, and vice versa. Garvey says it straight up - look guys we can boss up!!! We can pipe up on all fronts in all different types of industry, even military. We can do for ourselves and go back to our true homeland to create a reality far better than wondering if you are going to be the next hashtag on the news. He also says to those who don't want the reality he preached: "Enjoy being a slave to western materialism and culture. We don't desire anyone who is lazy and not cut out for the task at hand." Garvey was direct and straight to the point.

Those are the three main theories. My thing about that is this: why must the theories be at odds? Do they have to be at odds? I mean, can't I just focus on my followers and my constituents to lead and inspire them? Can I not focus on the people who agree with me and we build and become a spectacle to show others that this works. To the other guy - can't he do the same? I believe this is how we keep missing the mark in displaying true unity as Black Americans.

In spite of the Atlanta Compromise, which said that blacks should hold off on the political process while they focused on building their own for their families and communities, Booker T. secretly funded litigation and paid lawyer's fees for a few individuals who needed representation for unjust treatment under the law. This is the example of a perfect gentleman who really cares about the future of his race. He understood the value of "doing me". When you're so focused on "doing me", you don't have time or energy to spare on focusing on another person who is in all actuality working on your behalf as you are fighting for the same cause—the dignity of equality. He used his own personal funds to do these things all the while lobbying rich Caucasian philanthropists to help fund Tuskegee University. This gentleman, Booker T., was getting verbally dragged by prominent members of his race, who had tens of thousands of followers, and he never bickered back or stopped doing what he thought was best. I think Booker knew exactly what he was doing. He had a platform to do well and he refused to become someone he wasn't, as he didn't try to be fake toward whites or blacks. Booker T Washington spoke with logic and with passion to all people and his message was clear: black people are in dire need of education to live civilized lives and help build this country to be the best that it can be. Education is the key to less crime and peaceful understanding, especially after all the years of slavery. If you can see that I, Mr. Booker T. Washington, am an able bodied, intelligent individual worthy of your sympathy, then you can also see the 40 million others of my brothers and sisters in this land. They have the exact same ability and capacity for greatness even as I do.

That was Booker T.'s message and that's why I prefer his methods above the others, but I still share the other messages with all members of my race because they are all beneficial. These are the routes we must choose and we must do so in unity and harmony. Today the NAACP still employs many civil rights attorneys that help fight for the less fortunate and that is exactly what we're supposed to be doing regardless if the masses of the race hold on to other ideologies. I mean, Du Bois did word it correctly when he coined his *Talented Tenth* ideology. Yes, many members of the black race have become products of their environment, but we are sent to serve them and to play a role in the deliverance of their minds. You see, because of Booker T.'s message and strategy, he couldn't openly speak out in such bold ways against injustices occurring in the south. That wasn't his calling. Dubois, on the other hand, was in a better position to do something about it (which he did fight the good fight. My point is to say that I personally don't think it was or is beneficial for two black progressives to be at odds in such a public way). So the question is why can we not simply operate in harmony?

How interesting is it that we're discussing ideas, concepts, and events that were initiated over a 100 years ago that still impact us today. A house divided will not stand and the greatest illusion is separation. After the untimely deaths of Dr. Martin Luther King Jr. and Malcolm X, African-Americans have been without a definitive leader on a national scale. Actually, some say that we don't need black leaders rather we need black institutions. Well, I say we need strong black leaders, because strong black leaders build strong black institutions. We almost had a couple strong black leaders in my generation until they sabotaged themselves by not operating in truth and harmony for the race. Dr. Boyce Watkins and Dr. Umar Johnson, who were both on fire for the cause some years back, have lost their fervor and overall prestige in the eyes of the community at large when they came at odds with each other solely based off of pride. Still, there are black leaders among us within each community, and it is a must that we work together in harmony to build our communities to an economic strength. We can undoubtedly do all this in harmony and unison.

So here's the debate: who proposed the best method forward? Was it Booker T., Du Bois, or Garvey? Why? Now ask yourself - how am I applying the method I deem as superior in my own personal life? Am I working in harmony for the benefit of the race? Am I giving my due diligence? Not only do I personally believe in the value of debate, but I believe in the passion that all three of these gentlemen put into their ideology and their lifestyle as they only hoped for a better reality for all people. This is the type of information that we need to be feeding to our children, and these are the conversations that our adults need to be having. We have an enemy, that sometimes even lives next door, who threatens our very existence if ever they conjure up a reason to dislike any one of us as an individual at any given time. How best can we thwart that threat to minimize acts of hatred while maximizing the quality of life of everyone? How can I effectively turn a supposed known enemy into an ally?

While pursuing equity, equality, and personal liberty for oneself, family and community, understand that we all have the ability to choose the route we deem is best or a mixture thereof. Let's focus on Booker & Du Bois for a second. Now, there are black individuals who propose that the best way forward for Black America is found in each of us, as individuals, taking initiatives in our own personal lives to create a better path (Booker). Other African-Americans believe that the best way forward in creating sustainable change lies in continued aggressive political action (Du Bois). Personally, I think both options should work together in harmony, simultaneously even, without us trying to tear each other down. So first off—let's do both! Why not?

What is the end result that we hope to achieve as Black Americans? I'm not sure that there is a "one size fits all" answer for that question, as many of us have different expectations regarding our experiences or the lack thereof. However, in my view the end result should be true equity, equality, liberty, and freedom in every facet of life.

Legislative bills which violate the voting rights of African-Americans have been passed time and time again. Laws are supposed to protect innocent civilians, yet policies within police departments are constructed to provide high amounts of police presence in Black neighborhoods. Blacks then get arrested, charged, and convicted for crimes at an alarmingly disproportionate rate when compared to their white counterparts who commit the very same crimes at the same rates.

Blacks then disproportionately overpopulate the prison industry (naysayers: research the phrase disproportionate minority contact). Blacks come out of jail and prison to the same economic and living conditions and are now denied the ability to vote, attain certain careers, receive federal assistance for higher education, and so the same cycle continues. This is what is referred to as "the system". A system that was not created for African-American involvement or advancement; a system which literally guides everyone's daily lives in America. That system needs to be changed! Okay, yes . . . everyone knows this, but how?

I contend that African Americans must have the resolve to do and support BOTH! Participate in and support political action. Participate in and support continuous self-development for one's self and community as well. Each and every Black American must approach education with excitement! Education for ourselves and the same for our children! How else will we see the change that we would like to see? How do we attain the political goals and outcomes we seek if we do not, first, establish ourselves as stakeholders at the decision table? We must build our own and sustain our own with cooperative economics. We can start from where we are by spending our money with ourselves, which we normally would have spent outside the community. Those of us who are willing, and are in a position to do so, can depart from the traditional workforce once our own enterprise becomes sustainable. Still, the others who decide to stay in the traditional workforce can be our pillars of excellence who are championing our causes in industry and politics.

That's revolution! A sudden, complete, or marked CHANGE in one's life! In your life! A change in government and a system that oppresses the colored masses while exalting and holding guiltless privileged, fair skinned individuals with malice! If we only focus on self, then we might turn a blind eye to the systematic oppression that consumes black people by the masses. Should we choose to only focus on the systematic oppression, then we might forget to continuously sharpen up ourselves, families, and communities. We must be able to joyfully do both if we want to see a revolution and sustain the impacts of a revolution. This movement has already begun, but it takes you and I to maintain the momentum. It takes you and I to hold ourselves and our fellow brothers and sisters to the highest standards if we truly want to realize peace and freedom in America.

Are there black civil rights attorneys that can fight for us? Yes. Are there African-Americans interested in the police force that can top the ranks? Yes. Can I put a high emphasis on my child's education? Yes. Can I meet with friends, brainstorm, put our money together, and build a business? Yes. Can black people practice cooperative economics, just as other races do, and build a strong economic base whereby we become greatly valued, independent stakeholders on all issues black? Yes. And the answer to that last question is yes, not because of the color of our skin, but because of the color of currency (which might or might not be going crypto by the way). We can do these things! We can pursue excellence in every single area of life! Hell, it's not like some of us aren't doing these things now or that we have not done it before as a collective unit. The revolution has already begun!!! And we must do both to sustain it.

CHAPTER TWELVE

Of Adding Value

It took me a very long time to learn that there really is no such thing as failure, as long as you don't quit. If you make the conscious decision to quit then you have failed yourself. Other than that, everything else can be accepted as lessons learned. Throughout most of this book I've stated things that I've endured and areas I've triumphed in. I included the successes and setbacks as well as the depression that consumed me for about ten years due to placing too much focus on my failures. Today, however, I look back and analyze the way that God has been moving in my life and I see that all of those things were a part of my greater success story. Because I endured and kept moving forward, all aspects of my journey were there to help develop me into the person I am today. Again . . . there is no failure, there are only lessons learned. What I have found to be true is that distractions are inevitable, but if we continue to move forward then we can head to a better place.

President Obama's favorite president was Abraham Lincoln. Lincoln ran for office sixteen times and was defeated again and again, but he never allowed those defeats to cause him to be a failure. He continued to sharpen himself, he continued to endure, and he fought the good fight until he ultimately accomplished his goal of being elected to the highest office in the land. Actually, the original name of this book was going to be *Dreams From a Failure*, holding to the same concept of Lincoln and parodying President Obama's autobiography: *Dreams From My Father*. I was going to tell my life's story as I did now, but the main issue was that I was waiting for a great pinnacle of success prior to writing or releasing the book. Even up until 2018, I had the negative perception that I was a failure and that I couldn't laud myself as a success story until I had money to buy all the material things that I see advertised on television and in the lifestyle of the rich and famous. I was waiting until my company was breaking million dollar barriers (which will happen) before I felt that I had the authority to share my story. That is a faulty way of thinking, because today, I am a success. Today, I am doing the things that are necessary to ensure a better future and I am grateful for the many blessings that I have to experience today. There is no reason for depression or for a negative self-outlook. I now know that I am a success and the words that I have to share, today, are meaningful and can truly be useful to another person.

Along with the things that I have learned: knowing God and the universe that He placed me in, knowing more about who I am and my abilities to create and have dominion . . . . I now understand that I have the ability to be who I want to be and that I am in control of my destiny! This is the information that needs to be imparted to the next generation. We may feel jaded at times and we may feel marginalized, but we cannot make the choice to allow those feelings to have true power over our lives. This all begins in the mind. We can choose to allow others to have power over us or we can choose to create our own reality.

Practically every test that we face and every adverse emotion is part of the ongoing battle in our minds. The mind is where thoughts arise and are considered. Those thoughts give way to feelings and if those feelings are strong enough, they can turn into beliefs. Those beliefs have the power to do so many things, especially once spoken. Deep seated beliefs shape our paradigm and how we view the world, so one thing that must be noted is that words are extremely powerful. Again, the battle is for the mind.

Every event in life is trying to do two things:

1. Give you information
2. Sway or confirm your belief system.

A couple years ago my mentor and business partner Frank gave me the book *The Power of Now* and it was a very life changing guide for me. Through that book I learned that the mind is very powerful, and it's also geared towards negativity. If not placed in check, our brain will constantly dwell on negativity, so we have to force ourselves to think positively about things. Allow me to count my blessings for a second: I have two beautiful children who I love very much, they are fun to be around and they're well taken care of, I'm breathing, I'm able to help impact others in many ways, the sun is shining today, I saw beautiful clouds and awesome architecture on my way to the office, etc. So living in the present is where we can experience bliss. If we find that we're not where we thought we would be, then it's a good time to reconsider our strategy or switch up our focus.

What our mind does is create mental movies of the past which conjure up all types of emotions and, subsequently, affect our current state. The mind also operates in the manmade concept of time, so it can oftentimes make us anxious about milestones and timelines that we have set for ourselves. Have you ever found yourself saying, "I thought I would have accomplished XYZ by my 25th birthday?" How did that make you feel? Simply thinking about the past or the future can greatly alter your state, so living in the present is paramount. What the mind does is it disregards things that we may see that are positive, but it highlights even the slightest negative thing that may occur. So it's our job to be emotionally intelligent to notice negative feelings and to choose not to give in to it. Again, I've already shown how focusing on the past events caused me to be in a depressed state for ten years! What I should have done was acknowledge the particular feeling at the time and declare, "This particular situation made me angry", "This particular situation makes me sad", and "I do feel a certain way about it." Acknowledging negative emotions is very important. Acknowledge, but don't dwell. Use the negative emotion to think critically about how to address the issue you're facing and then, once you create a plan, you can revert back to the present moment and rest content while moving forward with living your best life.

Will you begin to call the things that are not as though they are? Do you believe that you can manifest your ultimate desires? Do you believe that you can be the change you wish to see in the world, your community, or household? Let's examine the story of Father Abraham from the Bible. Abraham is considered a patriarch solely because he had an incredible belief in God. God had required a lot of things of him and, every time He made a request, Abraham did it. The Bible says Abraham believed God and it was accounted to him for righteousness. Now I don't want to preach here, but most people who believe in God understands that he is Holy and set apart, and that in order to be considered righteous— one has to live a life without sinning. Now sinning is simply missing the mark in violating any one of the thousands of rules that life has set for us and the Bible clearly says that the unrighteous shall not enter heaven. However, Abraham believed God, and God declared him righteous simply for doing that. Belief is paramount.

Therefore it all boils down to the information that one has received and how it is processed in the mind. Science does not and cannot account for every facet under the sun, so the bottom line is that it is our faith that influences our belief system and subsequently determines how we live and view our lives. I'm not only referring to faith in a divine being, but faith in whatever information you receive in whatever form it is received in. Nevertheless, let's continue to examine religion for a moment. John 3:16, "For God so loved the world, that he gave his only begotten Son, that whosoever believes in Him shall not perish, but have everlasting life." Hundreds of millions of people believe they'll receive everlasting life simply because they BELIEVE it to be true. Also Romans 10:9 says, "If you confess with your mouth and believe . . . thou shalt be saved." BELIEF! I can't say this enough. There is a battle within us and that battle is for our mind and, ultimately, our faith. Typically when we reference faith we think God vs. Satan, or Christians vs. Muslims, or the devil working against me, etc. We tend to form our concept of faith *only* in that way when it's really a daily reality of affirmation. No weapon formed against me shall prosper! Says who? I speak it by faith and I'm certain! This gives the beliver confidence to move forward. "The just shall live by faith." "They overcame by the blood of the lamb and by the word of their testimony." All of the depression that I faced was based off of what was going on in my mind and the fact that I would not let go. God made Adam and Eve, and the serpent tempted them by saying what: "Yea, has God said that you shouldn't eat of the tree?" What was the enemy doing there? Casting doubt! But what does doubt do? It seeks to destroy your belief system. The battle is for the mind. So, whose report will you believe? Not only regarding God, but also about your own life. Who has control of your life? Can you do better? What is holding you back? It's all up to your belief system and, as the old cliché goes, "if you believe it then you can achieve it". Everything is based off of our mind and our faith.

When it comes to building the community, having the family that you desire, getting a new job or career, making a difference in the world, or doing anything you want to do . . . when you face opposition. . . do you believe that you can still accomplish your dreams? Will you believe in your ability to do what you want and witness the results that you want to see and, of course, that God has your back through it all?

You can do it, but it's all based on your faith and belief in your abilities to do so. The world is changing and there is still plenty of room for improvement and innovation. Although some may have experienced failure in certain areas, that doesn't mean you can't step into that area and add your influence to witness positive results and improvements. 2 Corinthians 6:14 tells us, "Don't be unequally yoked with unbelievers." Personally, I don't limit "unequally yoked" solely to my life partner being of a different religion. I equate it to belief in self! You can say that you're Christian or Muslim or Jewish, but if you don't believe in yourself and that you can accomplish things… you may have missed the mark. If you do not take steps to realize the things you desire, even though you have been thoroughly empowered by Scripture and all the wonderful things that it says about who you are, and if you lack belief in your abilities… you may be unequally yoked even within yourself. The unbeliever will always pull down the believer. The enemy in scripture has been called multiple names, but the one that stands out the most to me is the "accuser of the brethren." The enemy is an unbeliever who is there to weigh your psyche down with guilt and throw you off balance in hopes that you'll lack the faith to confidently move towards your goals.

You see, I know without a shadow of a doubt that when God looks at me, he sees the precious blood of His Son. He sees the sacrifice that he made over 2000 years ago and, yes, I make mistakes and miss the mark from time to time, but there is nothing that can eradicate the love that was shown through Christ and His redemptive sacrifice. You see, this is my personal belief and others have their own beliefs, but the point here is to be and remain solid on *your own* belief foundation. In the battle for the mind, the enemy wants to destroy your confidence towards God and make you feel as if you're alone. By the way, all religions, agnostic beliefs, and even Atheism are built on the foundation of faith. All religions and sciences stem from traditions, whether written or oral, that were passed down throughout the generations. Not one of us today can attest as an eye witness to any of the writings, nevertheless, we believe because it is solidified in our minds through faith.

Even when it comes to Christianity, I was taught at my school that the Bible is established by God and recognized by man. This is what's said to remove the human aspect that took place in establishing the canon or the books of the Bible. However, the story of Jesus has been simulated across many cultures and religions even before Jesus was born. This is true regarding virgin birth, the day his birthday is celebrated, the resurrection, the sanctity of his mother, and even the trinity concept. This is told through the Greek gods and the Egyptian gods Horus, Oasiris, and Isis which predates Christianity by thousands of years. Many hear of these stories and leave the faith, but Bible scholars claim that the enemy knew of Christ since the beginning of time, so he perpetuated many lies of false Christ's with similar storylines. Their position says the enemy did all this so that when the real One came we'd find ourselves in this predicament of utter confusion. You're at liberty to draw your own conclusions on the matter, but the point I'm trying to make here is that faith is key. I believe that God is attempting to get a hold of us through many means. He wants our attention. After He gets our attention we can see:

1. That he desires a relationship with us
2. He desires for us to live the best life we can while improving on what He created (making earth a better place)
3. He wants us to shine as lights so that other humans can desire to live the similar lifestyles

The only way we can do that is by operating in faith and believing that we can do so with confidence.

I just covered a lot of my personal beliefs about God and religion, but I want to make it clear that I also believe that religion is not necessary to achieve success. On the contrary, knowing the most about yourself and your abilities is what garnishes success. Psalm 73 proposes the question, "Why do the wicked prosper?" There were times when I would say to myself, "Why is it that I'm trying to do my best to live right, but I keep seeing others blatantly doing bad things and achieving better success than me?" The answer is simple: people achieve success because they affirm what they are about and that drives their daily decisions. Not only are people attracted to confidence and consistency, those values are key ingredients to garnishing success. When you make a stand to be about something, affirm your desires, and when you move on it—you are going to find success whether you want to do good or bad. So religion is not necessary for success.

******

In the ground there is oil. There are diamonds, gold, zinc, cobalt, and the lead that's used for a pencil. There are so many things found around us on this rich planet yet we don't know what to do with it until we receive the knowledge. Slaves didn't have the opportunity to trade or use the resources that were surrounding them in America because they were held captive and weren't allowed to read. Today, on the other hand, we have the power to receive vast amounts of information on practically any subject and create our own reality in today's age. It's not always going to be fun or easy, but we have the ability to achieve these things.

A Christian perspective holds that Jesus set us free from the strict rules of the past and gave us one main commandment: love your neighbor. How could it be so simple? Well, if you love someone then you're not killing them through malice, and you're not even abusing them. You're not deceiving them, sleeping with their wife, or doing anything that is missing the mark of simply loving them. You're not doing anything negative if you're practicing agape love. Will it always be reciprocated, no, but by this (love) men will know that we're God's disciples and by this— we can have a clear conscious towards the Creator. I believe this is what's needed to maintain inner balance and to witness the manifestation of our desires.

The Bible says, "In all things give thanks; for this is the will of God concerning your life." Here's the thread: contentment is smiled upon while complacency is frowned upon. Look at the children of Israel for instance. They were delivered from slavery in Egypt after 400 years of subjugation and cruel treatment. Once they got delivered, the first thing they did was complain at the first sight of distress (demonstrating a lack of faith in God and/or their abilities to overcome the situation). For what some may describe as a minor offense, the elders of that group were made to walk around in the wilderness in circles for 40 years. The story has it that God would not allow those who continually lacked faith (as demonstrated through complaining) to enter into the promise land. What promise or promises does God have on your life? What are your goals or where are you trying to make it to? The promises of God are "yea and amen", meaning, yes chase after your dreams . . . He has your back. Go create your reality! So long as you're creating within His will (love) then He has your back. But actively choosing not to operate in love and not being grateful can cause you to not be in harmony with the Creator (or Universe if you so choose), hurt your balance within yourself, and cause you not to receive the things that you ultimately desire. I find it to be that simple. If you're operating in love and gratitude then you're in tune with the Most High and you're vibrating on the highest frequency possible to accomplish your mission.

Booker T. Washington says you'll never gain a friend by insulting them and, in the book *How To Win Friends and Influence Others*, it states that everyone thinks that they are right and no one ever wants to be called out. Ever! The book even describes how the notorious crime lord Al Capone was shocked and appalled when he was finally convicted to go to prison despite the fact that he had orchestrated the killings of hundreds of people. No one wants to have the finger pointed at them even if they are dead wrong, so how can we bridge gaps and build communities? By setting the standard of love, that's how. When you have a clear conscious to where you want to go and when you know that God is on your side - you can find better ways to address issues by doing your best to operate in the spirit of love. Walking in love and gratitude is also the fast track to attaining happiness. In America, we've been endowed by our creator with life, liberty, and the pursuit of happiness. I say there is no longer a need to *pursue* when the blue print has been laid out on how to *attain*. Continue moving forward with your goals and dreams for your family and future; remain focused in the present moment. When you do that then you can rest content knowing that the future is bright.

As distractions come, understand that they're just distractions and that you don't live based off of the temporary things that your eyes are observing. You call into action what you want. Believe that amazing and outstanding things are coming your way. Reflect on how the journey has prepared you for this present moment. Realize your newfound strength and newfound wisdom due to the enduring of whatever happened in the past. Love and gratitude helps us to champion the battle for our mind and, I believe, this is the key to everything in life. I may be dreaming, but with love and gratitude we can witness a world without prejudice and racism, a life without having to look over our shoulders, we can free ourselves from negative strongholds that bind our brains, and we can loose ourselves from the spirit of anxiety and depression. This is also what I believe to be the key to world peace. Although it appears simple and minor, love and gratitude is how you maintain a clear conscience and have the wherewithal to work in tandem with the Creator as you achieve all of your desires. This is what we learn through the law of attraction which is similar to the concept of Karma that most have heard of. You get what you put out to the world in word and in deed. Indeed. When you say or do positive things, you emit a frequency that goes out into the universe and, just like magnet, the universe draws in the things that you emit. If you live in a world, even in your head, when you have to fight against people, notions, and establishments then that will be your reality. When you choose love then that becomes your reality as well. It becomes the default way to how you will view life, and you learn how to best respond to the journey by faith. This emboldens your happy state and your faith in the Creator as well as your mission on earth. The end result is a fulfilled life. We can witness the things we want to see in the world but, it begins with us being the change we wish to see on the individual level.

In fact, I believe it should be the overall mission of every community to help its members attain self-actualization.

Self-actualization is where you begin to thoroughly examine yourself, look back on all that you've been able to accomplish and begin to contemplate how much more you are able to do. In a sense, it's the place where you've become more in tune with yourself and you find that you are pretty self-sufficient. You begin to reflect on your accomplishments and become more in tune with the greatness that lies within you. If you're able to reach the level of self-actualization you will see that, along your journey, you have created your own systems and mastered multiple ways of getting your needs met.

In the groups that I conduct with my clients, I have them jot down five of their greatest failures or setbacks and five of their greatest successes. What we find every time is that they realize, no matter how much pain they've experienced along the way, they're here today and they've experienced times of great joy and great pleasure at different times along the journey as well. This gives the wherewithal to forecast into the future and say, it doesn't matter what comes my way. They now understand that they can accomplish anything. Now my clients begin to view obstacles as a non-threat, because they understand their own greatness and that Providence is working on their behalf. They're "self-actualized" in that they know more about themselves and their abilities. This is why we have to come up from the trap, because trap culture is hardly talking about positive things. It's hardly causing people to think outside of the box in terms of innovation and living the best, most successful, and crime free life! It's not calling you to create change, it's not calling you to realize who you are, and trap culture is most certainly not calling you to do something new.

Johari's Window: Picture a square window with four equal sized window panes. The top left pane is pane one, the top right is pane two, bottom left is pane three, and the bottom right pane is the fourth and final pane.

Pane one: your perception of yourself. This pane reveals the way you see yourself and what you know about yourself that others possibly don't see or know.

Pane two: This pane is how others see and perceive you, but you might not always agree or see things that way. For instance, have you ever been called a jerk, but felt that the other person was the one in the wrong? It may be a time for self-reflection (that's the high route right?). Now, maybe it's true or maybe it's not, but the point is that you don't necessarily see yourself like that.

In the third pane you have certain things that you know about yourself and you also will allow others to know as well. For example, it could be a quality or a hobby displaying that you are passionate about saving stray dogs in the community. For me personally, those who know me understand that I have a publishing company and that I care about the future of the world at large with special attention given to issues impacting the African Diaspora and all marginalized and disenfranchised people across the globe.

Now, pane four is called the unknown. We don't know what lies there. We might find out later on, but ultimately, the unknown is unlimited potential to do incredible things: *positive or negative*. They say man is afraid of the unknown, but have you ever considered that there is greatness lying inside of you that you have not even tapped into yet? There is inconceivable, dynamic potential that can either be channeled for great good or great evil. That potential lies within each and every one of us.

Here's an example of the unknown from a negative perspective. Have you ever found yourself in a situation you never thought you'd be in and you ended up doing extreme hurt to another or even yourself? All was fine until one day a certain event occurred and you ended up responding in ways you never would have expected or calculated. This is the cry of many who sit behind bars for homicide charges and many lost souls who inadvertently took their own lives. Great potential resides within each and every one of us. What about *Black Spider Man*, Mamoudou Gassama, of Mali? As a positive example of the unknown, this gentleman witnessed a baby hanging from a balcony on the 5th floor of a building in France, and there was no resolution in sight. With a burst of resolve and instinct, Mamoudou was able to tap into his inner greatness and scale the multiple story building. He climbed the building similar to a spider, pulled himself to the 5th floor, and he rescued the young kid who was previously facing death. Black Spiderman tapped into the unknown. Clearly he had a heart and a care for humanity, but he also used his natural ability to do something that he never imagined doing in his life.

You never know what you're capable of doing and this is why we must always seek to be the greatest version of ourselves every day. On a regular day, Black Spider Man never would have thought about climbing a building, but when an opportunity came to do something good. . . he stepped out and made the impossible happen all while risking his own life. Now, I'm not saying go out and risk your life!! But I'm saying that you should love yourself, believe in yourself and your abilities, continuously work on personal growth, and practice positive affirmations. You will begin to see supernatural changes. You will become happier, more fulfilled, and your desires will be drawn to you like a magnet.

CHAPTER THIRTEEN

Last Words

I've always wanted to write an autobiography, not to be vainglorious, but because I wanted to tell my story to people who had less fortunate experiences in life such as I had. As stated in the previous chapter, I was actually waiting until I became successful to write this book, or until I felt that I was at the pinnacle of success. In other words, I was waiting for the day I could be happy with the great shape of my finances. I never could bring myself to writing a sentence until I switched the title around which happened shortly after I read *Up From Slavery* by Booker T. Washington. Change your story; change your life. The sum total of my life's journey has taught me that the time is always now. If you wait for the perfect timing, perfect place, perfect scenario then you'll never move into action because those elements rarely ever come together. Time waits for no man and there is never a wrong time to do the right thing. You have to start putting things into motion and things will begin to take shape and manifest. Even right now with my middle class status in America, God is working out miracles through the words being written here and through Melanin Origins; the world is witnessing the manifestation.

Through the chapters of this book we have demonstrated that the root of the trap is based in drug dealing, which points back to a drug house where addicts go to receive their drugs. This could be a house, hotel, apartment, abandoned building, or even a vehicle. It's normally a free and open space where people can receive their drugs, do their drugs, and sometimes even hang out until they realize that they need another fix. Popular culture, within Black Culture, has taken the negatively rooted word, trap, and glamorized that type of lifestyle along with all the illegal things that's associated with it. Drugs were once used as a tool of the American Government to destroy the inner cities and our communities, but now drug dealing is the root of trap culture! So now we have trap music, trap fashion, trap instruments, trap karaoke (which I understand is fun), trap yoga . . . I'm using my position to merely suggest that maybe we could change the verbiage and call it something different. Put different content in the music, because this is not the way. Our mindsets must reflect our lifestyle and knowing that we are dealing with a known enemy, white supremacy, we need to be more strategic with the messages that we disseminate to our people and to the world at large.

Building off the root of the trap, which is drug dealing, we discussed the micro effect which is when we come to internalize trap culture. Individuals who were brought up in environments where this lifestyle is prevalent are at the greatest risk of internalizing it or owning it as their way of life. They believe that this is the way life is supposed to be and so they act accordingly. On one hand they have society telling them to believe in themselves, obey the law, strive for success, that they can accomplish their dreams all throughout grade school through many prosocial mediums. On the other hand, they have the antisocial norms of their environment telling them something different and painting a different picture of how life is supposed to be. These individuals walk around confused up until they take a bold stance about which direction they will go in life and, while dealing with systematic oppression, it's easier to choose the lower hanging fruit of *trap*. Understandably so, but now is the time to act in coming up from the trap.

The macro effect or external aspect of the trap is that - we are not the ones who put ourselves in this position from the beginning. A lot of money goes into the music industry to influences this type of culture; there is a system in place. The radio executives will blot out anti-Semitic references, as they should. They won't play songs advocating violence to police entities, as they shouldn't. However, they see no issue with fully blasting lyrics about killing black men, selling drugs, date raping women, kidnapping children, etc. on predominately black media outlets and, of course, this is not the thread on predominately Caucasian media outlets. Is this because the executives want to keep us inundated with these violent images of ourselves? Is it because they are trying to help poor African-Americans get rich through rapping so they can help their families out of poverty? I contend that there is a strategic plan laid out, primarily based on greed, that uses African-Americans as pawns while not even giving one damn about the detrimental consequences. It's a gamble they are willing to take against black lives, but they aren't willing to take that same gamble on any other group of people. It's on us to recognize this malice and come up from the trap.

To the trap rappers who will argue this point, "I'm just speaking on my reality". You're not just speaking, you're endorsing and celebrating. It's one thing to speak on negative things that you see, have seen or experienced, but it's another thing to glamorize, celebrate and prescribe that type of behavior to others. You have executives who don't look like you and tell you that you'll find success when you talk about these things . . . again; *he who has the gold makes the rules.* Just as "the system" creates legislation to target African-American communities with police presence, criminalize their everyday behavior, and disproportionately arrest, convict, and kill them... these are the same tactics the music industry uses. That's the external aspect. Trap music and culture is a problem. Not only that, but many artist end up getting 360 deals and end up being poor and in the streets again left to fend for themselves. Many end up depressed and even hauled off to jail or prison for their actions.

We must come up from the trap because we must save our children. We need to strengthen our communities. We must fully overcome the vicious cycle of poverty, the school to prison pipeline, mass incarceration, and the lack of access to opportunity. Knowing who we are gives us the wherewithal to sustain ourselves economically and financially. It better positions us to focus on our own households, building businesses, and cleaning up our neighborhoods. And everyone benefits from keeping the hood clean. No one is at a loss when we can look our brothers and sisters in the face with a smile and shake their hand. Today, we are in a prime position to change and strengthen our communities. We can get in the police force, live in the neighborhood of our choice, and advocate for that community against inequitable practices. We can become civil rights attorneys, non-profit executives, and we can have a unified front. We can start gun clubs for recreational purposes and for community protection.

One of my favorite women in history, the late Ida B. Wells, is widely known and celebrated for her excellence in journalism and for her anti-lynching campaigns. She once had friends who owned a black owned pharmacy whose competitor was across the street from them, a white owned business. In the process of time, there was a conflict between the two entities due to the success of the black store. The conflict escalated into a physical altercation whereby one of the white members ended up getting killed in the commotion, so the police came and immediately took the black store owners to jail. On that very same night a white mob stormed in the jail where the black store owners were being held, broke in, and killed those black business owners who, initially, were merely defending themselves against white aggression directed at their business. So here it is that I'm talking about coming up from the trap, saying who we are and what we can be, but history shows us again and again what can happen to us when we aspire for greatness. I can't sit here and act as if evil, atrocious things don't happen to us when we try to live our best lives according to sincerity and truth. A similar story is told of Black Wall Street in Tulsa where a whole town was booming and rich being filled with black lawyers, business men, postal workers, and ultimately—self-sufficiency. The American government bombed the entire town due to "riots" that took place once envious Caucasian aggressors brought trouble to the town. Imagine that. The actual government literally dropped bombs on its own citizens even before Hiroshima, Japan. For some reason, collective black progress is seen as a threat.

The Bureau of Justice, which turned into the FBI, is responsible for the dissemination of all progressive black movements (COINTELPRO) whose sole purpose was to protect us from these types of situations and provide for our economic and moral development. They took down Marcus Garvey, Malcolm X, and the Black Panther Movement which brought us many influential individuals including Fred Hampton and Huey P. Newton. The CIA even declassified their conspiracy to kill Dr. Martin Luther King Jr., which they were successful in accomplishing. The government kills our leaders, disrupts our progress, and creates systems to impress economical and psychological damage on us. This is what they do when we are trying to lead our people to be successful. It beats us down so much that we feel that we have to succumb to their wiles and only live in the reality that they create for us. At the end of the day, we still have two options here: do we lie dormant or do we stand up as men (able-bodied individuals) ready to pipe up on all fronts. All fronts. When I say gun club, I'm serious. Not to advocate violence but to demonstrate skill and tact and to be a stronghold for the community against evil. When I say black businesses and nonprofits, I mean creating and supporting organizations that will heal and stimulate the community. I'm talking about providing jobs and a healthy means of living as well as restoring drug addicts and broken people. This vision involves enhancing services at community centers and essentially being fathers for the fatherless and mothers for the motherless.

We must come up from the trap and realize that we are fearfully and wonderfully made. We have the spirit of God living inside us. We can emit frequencies and bend the universe to our will by the things we speak and believe. If you don't know that about yourself then you're the perfect candidate for the system. That's the type of person they want to manipulate. They don't want people who know the abilities they possess. They don't want people who know and understand who they are. They don't want people who realize that infinite intelligence is within them, abundantly. I want my people to know that we can master radio waves, introduce the latest technological advances like our ancestors did, and we are capable of many more great things that we can do when we put our minds to it. It is said that man uses less than 10% of his brain capacity; we are able to tap into the fourth pane in Johari's window and explore the unknown. This is not privy or limited to any race, gender, or ethnicity, but it is limited to mankind. No other being has what we have to subdue, conquer, and use all of this to our benefit. We're barely scratching the surface of God's great creation, of which, the human eye is only able to view less than 1% of the electromagnetic spectrum. Understanding the depths of this place where God has placed us and our ability to have power over it all is how we can come up from the trap and witness the changes that we want to see in our individual lives, families, and communities.

If you haven't noticed by now, Booker T. Washington is my favorite historical figure. His motto was - let's gather ourselves together so we can build among ourselves and better our economic condition. We can have positive interactions with other races while remaining focused on what we need to do for ourselves. Let's put our best foot forward to live a respectful life and build our community. If we address Caucasians about full equality right now, we may not be able to handle the repercussions, so let's not provoke them by demanding full equity right now, but as time progresses and as they see us faring well, they'll eventually see and believe us to be equals. Many people found problems with Booker's message (remember this was over 100 years ago and he was talking to people who were not too far removed from the years of slavery), but Booker T. Washington was able to find great success in the south and as a national leader. As for today, we're in the best place we've ever been. The U.S. constitution is on our side and that's what every decent law and governmental body is supposed to stand on. Therefore, we can rise to the ranks in government and industry, set precedents, take down corrupt laws and law officials, and we can base everything on the principles written in 1776: "We believe these things to be true..."

Too many cultured and intelligent brothers and sisters are spread throughout the whole world and we're in the best position to do the most for ourselves, but we're caught up in this trap and we must come out of it. I'm reminded of my good friend Tamesha Berryman from Oak Cliff, Texas who worked two jobs to support her daughter while she continued her education in the medical field. Tamesha began as a Certified Nurse's Assistant, became certified as a Licensed Vocational Nurse, continued on to get her Bachelor's degree in Nursing, passed the Registered Nurse exam, and landed her dream job working for the county hospital in the labor department. She refused to believe that she was a product of her environment and she created a better reality for herself. Now she even has her own business catering fruit trays to local businesses. She's a shining example of what happens when we come up from the trap. She's living the life she wants to live and what's even better than that, Tamesha is now in a place where she can influence policies and procedures if there is ever a need for improvement at her place of employment. We all can rise to the ranks, and once we get there what will we do? Secure finances and create equitable change.

When the United States and China are at odds, they start issuing sanctions and tariffs against one another. I contend that that's the same way we have to operate was a community as well. One of our sanctions is boycotting, effective boycotting. In the year 2018, African-Americans have over 1.7 trillion dollars of buying power whereby we could bankrupt industries simply by not participating. We can vote people out of office and we can vote people into office, as we demonstrated in 2017 when the Alabama Senate went from a red (Republican) state to a blue (Democrat) state for the first time in history due to an extremely high African American voter turnout (yes, black women did seize the day). There is so much that we can do, but it's on us to come up from the trap.

I close with an excerpt from Booker T. Washington's Atlanta Compromise:

"A ship lost at sea for many days suddenly sighted a friendly vessel. From the mast of the unfortunate vessel was seen a signal, "Water, water; we die of thirst!" The answer from the friendly vessel at once came back, "Cast down your bucket where you are." A second time the signal, "Water, water; send us water!" ran up from the distressed vessel, and was answered, "Cast down your bucket where you are." And a third and fourth signal for water was answered, "Cast down your bucket where you are." The captain of the distressed vessel, at last heeding

the injunction, cast down his bucket, and it came up full of fresh, sparkling water from the mouth of the Amazon River. To those of my race who depend on bettering their condition in a foreign land or who underestimate the importance of cultivating friendly relations with the Southern white man, who is their next-door neighbor, I would say: "Cast down your bucket where you are"— cast it down in making friends in every manly way of the people of all races by whom we are surrounded."

I have used personal stories from my life in an attempt to demonstrate how many people of color share similar experiences and how I came up from the trap. I opened up in vulnerability and told how I beat depression and my long journey of how, through knowledge of self, the application of history, and the law of attraction, I discovered the blueprint for community empowerment: collective prosperity and individual happiness. To those of my race who have a desire to live their best life in peace, happiness, and prosperity, to those who are filled with concerns of the welfare of their families and communities, to those beautifully, courageous members of my race who simply want the next generation to not experience anything that we have endured in our past – "Cast down your bucket where you are". Cast it down into the deep rich soil that produces oil, gold, diamonds, and minerals which produce electricity and births new technologies such as the internet and smart phones. You were given dominion over the earth to use every aspect of it to your greatest ability. As Booker T. Washington further stated, "cast it down in making friends in every manly way of the people of all races by whom we are surrounded." There is no fear in love, but perfect love casts out fear and as much as lies within you – live peaceably among all men. Cast down, I say, Cast down your bucket right from where you are because you were born with an innate ability to impact change in this world! We have the power to create our reality. Build your dreams: brick by brick.

Bibliography

Adaso, H. (2017, March 18). "The History of Trap Music"
Retrieved February 10, 2019 from
<https://www.thoughtco.com/history-of-trap-
music-2857302>

Bialik, K. (2018, February 22). "5 facts about blacks in
the U.S." Retrieved February 10, 2019 from
<http://www.pewresearch.org/fact-
tank/2018/02/22/5-facts-about-blacks-in-the-u-s/>

Elkins, K. (2018, March 13). "Here's how much money
middle-class families earn in every US state"
Retrieved February 10, 2019 from
<https://www.cnbc.com/2018/03/13/how-much-
money-middle-class-families-earn-in-every-us-
state.html>

GUSTAVO LÓPEZ, NEIL G. RUIZ, and EILEEN
PATTEN. (2017, September 8). "Key facts
about Asian Americans, a diverse and growing
population." Retrieved February 10, 2019
from <http://www.pewresearch.org/fact-
tank/2017/09/08/key-facts-about-asian-
americans/>

(Ladson-Billings, 1994). Culturally Responsive Teaching. Brown University.

NCAA. (n.d.). Retrieved February 10, 2019 from <www.ncaa.org / www.norwichcsd.org/ Downloads/ProSportsOdds.doc>

Rudwick, E. (2019, February). W.E.B. Du Bois American Sociologist and Social Reformer .Britannica. Retrieved February 10, 2019 from <https://www.britannica.com/topic/Talented-Tenth>

Social Security Online. "Wage Statistics for 2018" Retrieved February 10, 2019 from <https://www.ssa.gov/cgi-bin/netcomp.cgi?year=2018>

Paulo Coelho. *The Alchemist*, 1988.

The Editors of Encyclopedia Britannica (n.d.). Retrieved February 10, 2019 from <https://www.britannica.com/topic/Universal-Negro-Improvement-Association.>

University of California, Davis. (2017, September 13). "What are the poverty thresholds today?" Retrieved February 10, 2019 from https://poverty.ucdavis.edu/faq/what-are-poverty-thresholds-today